MAX HAINES

CRIME FLASHBACK

The Toronto Sun Publishing Corporation
Limited,
333 King Street East, Toronto, Ontario
Canada M5A 3X5

Illustrated by Risto Turunen and Andy Donato

Edited by Linda A. Fox

Manufactured in Canada by Webcom Limited

ISBN 0-919233-00-7

For: Susan, Maureen, and Eleanor

CONTENTS

PART 4 POT POURRI

Max Haines was born in the peaceful little town of Antigonish, Nova Scotia. His fascination with true crime dates back to his youth when he studied criminal behavior as a hobby.

Haines' nationally syndicated column "Crime Flashback" appears each week in the Toronto Sun and the Toronto Sunday Sun. He has appeared on scores of television and radio talk shows across the country, spinning his unique brand of the strange and unusual in the field of crime.

Max resides in Etobicoke, Ontario, with his wife Marilyn and three daughters, Susan, Maureen and Eleanor. He is a gentle soul.

FOREWORD

The forty individual criminal cases presented to you between these covers were written over a period of years. Because of this readers might find a marked difference in writing style from one horrendous happening to the other. Then again, there is a distinct difference in mood between researching the tragic murder of an innocent lady in rural Ontario (Who Killed Mrs. Henning?) and basking in the sun in Jamaica after touring what was once the largest plantation in the country (The White Witch of Rosehall).

Please forgive me if tiny tidbits of humor occasionally have been allowed to find their way into what otherwise are dastardly or at least dishonest deeds. I just can't help getting a chuckle out of a man who managed to make a million out of goat glands (The Goat Gland Caper) or an aristocratic gentleman who sold the Eiffel Tower twice (Anybody Want to Buy the Eiffel Tower?).

Here they are for better or worse. Put out the cat. Lock the door. Turn on the lamp and pull up the covers. You are about to cuddle up with a good crook.

PART 1

THE POISONERS

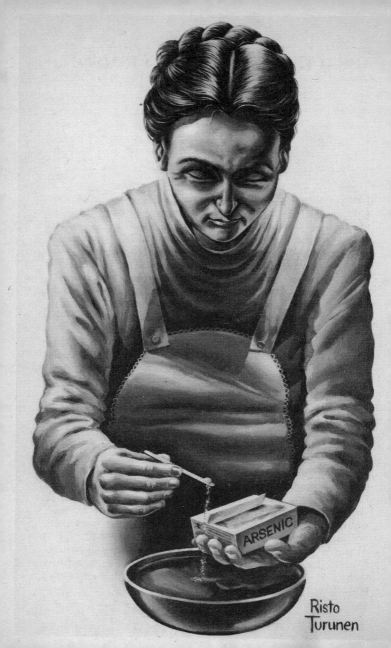

PEACHES, CREAM AND POISON

I have always maintained that poisoners, as a group, are the most cowardly of all murderers. They have at their disposal the ability to divorce themselves completely from their victim as the end draws near.

In France, back in the days of Louis XIV, poisoning was such a common occurrence that many potential victims let their pets have a generous helping of porridge before partaking themselves. There were more dead dogs in France at that time than there were snuffboxes.

It was quite in order for the common folk, like you or me, to administer poison to a rich parent or an unwanted lover, but heavens, that would never do for the aristocracy. No, nothing could be more uncouth. The killer managed to be twice removed from the victim. Here is how it worked.

The practice of poisoning became so fashionable that certain apothecaries, better known as pharmacists here in Canada, became well known for their ability to mix up a fatal powder in whatever strength the occasion called for. These dispensers of custom-made poisons only dealt with an elite group who administered poison. There were only about two dozen top notch poisoners in all of Europe. Like specialists in many fields today, their fees were atrocious, but the results were guaranteed.

A member of the aristocracy of France would turn over a large sum of money to the poisoner with explicit instructions as to how the deed was to be carried out, then sit back and wait for the funeral.

Now that we have established the ground rules, I would like you to meet Madame Marie de Brinvilliers, an aristocratic lady who was to become one of France's extraordinary poisoners, if not the all time champ.

Marie was born to many of the finer things of life. Her father was a wealthy government official, who saw to it that the apple of his eye attended the best private schools and generally led a life in keeping with her social standing. As if all this wasn't enough, Marie was a stunning looker, with a voluptuous figure.

Baron Antoine de Brinvilliers was the son of another highly placed government official. He was a handsome devil, who did credit to his French Army officer's uniform. The lovely Marie and the dashing Antoine became lovers and were married.

All was not peaches and cream. Heavens no. You see, both the Baron and Baroness had one thing in common. They both slept around whenever the opportunity presented itself. The records of the old case hint that right after the marriage ceremony Marie saw fit to dispense a sexual favor to one of the church officials in the vestry.

Everyone has their own moral standards. Who are we to judge? Both Marie and Antoine seemed to condone each other's promiscuous dalliances, but the situation was nevertheless a potentially explosive one. Antoine had received a large dowry from Marie's daddy, which he promptly blew on gambling and other ladies.

At just this susceptible moment, Antoine became friends with a man called Godin. It was a mistake. Godin was no sooner under Antoine's roof than he made himself comfortable under Marie's sheets. Godin and Marie became lovers, and it is certain that their affair was carried on so openly that Antoine knew that something was rotten in the State of Denmark.

Whereas Antoine didn't seem to mind the shenanigans going on in his house, Marie's aged father was furious. He arranged to have Godin arrested and thrown into the Bastille, which from early descriptions can only be compared to Toronto's Don Jail as a place where one would not care to stay for an extended period of time. While thus detained, Godin met another character, named Exile, an apothecary whose specialty it was to make nasty little white powders which killed. Wouldn't you know it, Godin and Exile became good friends while passing the time of day in the Bastille.

When both men were released, Godin provided Exile with

a home in return for all the little secrets of the poisoner's trade. He passed along these juicy tidbits to his mistress, Marie. Why, you might ask, did Marie want such information? Because her ever loving daddy was becoming a nuisance, that's why. It was getting so that a girl couldn't hit the hay with whomever she desired. Besides, daddy had all that lovely cash, just when hubby Antoine was running short. Daddy had to go.

Immediately after the lovers made their momentous decision Daddy came down with a rather mysterious malady. His loving daughter was at his bedside throughout, but it was no use. After a short but painful illness, Daddy died.

Marie went wild. She had money, a husband, a lover, or should we say lovers; for Marie, the passionate one, did not confine her horizontal activities exclusively to Godin.

The path of true love never runs smooth. Now, Marie's two brothers objected to her way of life. Impetuously, one day, she dashed off a note to Godin which said, in essence: Quick, get out the powders. Marie, in her haste for results, broke one of my hard and fast rules for murderers. Never, but never, commit anything to paper. Godin told Marie that it would take a great deal of money to hire a professional poisoner. Then he tucked away Marie's note for safekeeping.

The de Brinvilliers' social circle was shocked by the sudden demise of Marie's two brothers. She was really rolling now. Marie figured poisoning was the answer to any problem. Her husband was a bore, and she thought it might be a good idea for him to be removed permanently from the scene. A by-product of this not so original idea would be her marriage to Godin.

Now, our friend Godin was no fool. He knew that Marie was no longer his private domain. Besides, how would he ever be able to enjoy breakfast, never being sure whether there was a little white powder in his cafe au lait.

Without warning, Godin died. His death was not considered to be murder, so we will never know whether or not Marie slipped him a little something, out of anger. His belongings revealed incriminating letters from Marie, particularly the one describing how she wanted her brothers poisoned post haste.

Once the cat was out of the bag, it became necessary for Marie to leave Paris hurriedly. She entered a convent in

Liege, using a fictitious name. For three years Marie was confined to the convent, which must have been comparable to cutting a mouse off from his cheese supply.

When her real identity was discovered, she was arrested. She was carrying a detailed confession of her crimes, which she had written while in the convent.

Marie didn't fare well. In her time, torture was prevalent in France, and she was beaten and burned in an effort to get her to reveal all the lurid details of her past life.

Marie de Brinvilliers was finally beheaded for her crimes.

LOVE AND LETHAL LUNCHES

If you ever plan on hastening a friend's or relative's demise by adding a touch of poison to their food, there are certain rules which even the most impulsive must observe. It's only basic common sense to place the poison in the proper food and, for goodness sake, be certain the right person consumes the laced goodies. Theresa Wasserleben and her mummie, Maria Godau, observed the former rule but were decidedly negligent in complying with the latter.

Maria, still a fine cut of a woman in her early forties, had been thoroughly embarrassed when some question arose as to how her late husband had expired. It seemed simple enough to Maria. One fine day back in Cottage Hill, Alabama, Hubby Godau suffered severe tummy cramps. The stomach trouble became more severe until the poor gentleman curled up and died. Nothing could be more straightforward, thought Maria. It was ulcers, or bladder trouble, or something—take your pick.

Busybodies, such as police and medical authorities, disagreed. Those suspicious souls kept insisting that it was murder by poison. Finally, to clear up the entire matter, Maria went through the rather tiring experience of standing trial for murder. Her insistence that it was all a mistake was borne out. Maria was acquitted.

But that was all behind the closely knit mother and daughter team. Now, two years later, Maria thought it best for all concerned if her impetuous and extremely well stacked daughter Theresa entered the matrimonial sweepstakes. The card Theresa drew from the deck was a giant of a man who answered to the tongue twister of Freidrich Wasserleben. He also came running if you shouted Freddie.

Freddie tipped the scales at 250 lbs. and stood 6 foot 3

inches in his hand-knit stockinged feet. The apple strudel of
Theresa's eye hailed from Hamburg, Germany. He had has-
tened to leave there as a teenager in order to join the German Navy. After his discharge from the Navy in 1893, Freddie migrated to America and settled down in Mobile, Ala.
Here, at a dance, the 44-year-old stevedore met 18-year-old
Theresa. Freddie took one look at the long-legged, more
than amply endowed Theresa and said, "That's for me."
Theresa had very few objections and Maria, sitting on the
sidelines, had absolutely none.

As they say in the story books, in due course the couple
were wed, and went dashing away on their honeymoon.
Now, folks, you have to keep an eye on those mothers-in-
law. Freddie assumed that he and his brand new wife would
be bedding down in his cozy apartment. He assumed wrong.
While the lovebirds were away cooing, or whatever, Maria
moved all their belongings into her home. An exhausted
Freddie returned from his honeymoon to find out that he
would be living under his mother-in-law's roof. At first he
objected; but once it was pointed out how much more
cheaply three could live than two, he consented to the surprise living arrangements.

The surprises were just beginning. Maria informed Freddie that she had bought him a waterfront saloon. Now that
wasn't hard to take, thought Freddie. Anything was better
than the stevedore business. Big Freddie, with all those mus-
cles, loved dishing out the suds down at the saloon.

Meanwhile, Maria wasn't finished with the surprises. One
frosty Friday, Freddie closed up the saloon and came directly home, as was his habit. Instead of Theresa rushing to
the door to meet him, he was confronted by Maria, who
informed him that Theresa had gone to Birmingham to visit
a friend for a few days.

As Maria so subtly put it, "What the hell, let's make the
most of it." She initiated the festivities by opening a bottle of
schnapps, which put Freddie in the mood for bigger and
better things. Folks, it embarrasses me to have to relate to
you that Freddie and his mother-in-law made their way to
the sleeping quarters. Oh, what's the use. They jumped into
the sack and didn't come up for air for two days. From this
brief interlude on, Freddie became lover to both his wife and
his mother-in-law on a more or less permanent basis.

Other matters concerned the menage-a-trois. Let's face it,

Freddie, while he may have been super in the stud business, left a lot to be desired when it came to dispensing suds. The saloon went broke.

Freddie, demonstrating his well known ability to bounce back, joined the Mobile police department. Maria was elated at the news. With her customary eye for the future, she took out a nice fat insurance policy on Freddie's life. As far as Maria was concerned, Freddie became a walking, talking, $15,000 on the hoof. You couldn't be too careful. After all, police work could be dangerous.

Freddie turned out to be a darned good cop. He apprehended his share of drunks and thieves, but darn the luck, he never got as much as a scratch in the line of duty. Years went by. Everyone liked the big, good natured cop. In fact, when Freddie was on night duty, he got in the habit of checking up on ladies whose husbands he knew were out of town. Some of those ladies were so grateful, they invited Freddie into their homes for an hour or six to partake of horizontal fun and games. Freddie was always willing to serve and protect. What with the string of ladies on the night shift and Maria and Theresa at home, the now 50-year-old Freddie was almost always in a state of exhaustion.

There comes a point in every little tale of sex and mayhem when someone has to make a decision. Now was that time. Maria and Theresa decided to murder Freddie. Fifteen thousand fresh crisp dollar bills were more desirable than one exhausted Freddie.

The mother and daughter team were in the habit of packing a lunch for the breadwinner before he went on the night shift. How convenient, thought Maria, as she liberally laced the lunch with arsenic. The two little devils stayed up all night waiting for word of Freddie's death. Nothing happened. As the sun rose over Mobile, Freddie came whistling up the front walk, big as life and twice as cheerful. He didn't even have a suggestion of a tummy ache.

Something had gone wrong. Theresa said to Maria, "Don't worry, Mamma, if at first you don't succeed, try, try again. We will poison Freddie tomorrow." Well, folks, there were many tomorrows, all of which were followed by that infuriating Freddie whistling up the front walk.

Now, Freddie had no idea he was being poisoned. For months the ladies he would visit always made him a nice light snack. He never ate the lunches Maria and Theresa prepared. In fact, he got in the habit of splitting his lunch with four or five of his fellow cops. Some took ill, but no-one ate his entire lunch so that their intake of arsenic was never fatal. On some occasions Freddie would just toss the poisoned lunch into the garbage. He always noted what was in his lunch, as Maria and Theresa had developed the annoying habit of questioning him about it. He was always quick to compliment them, although he never ate a bite.

While all this was going on, the two ladies were becoming impatient. One night they decided to hurry things along. Freddie was asleep in the very bed which had seen so much action in the past. Maria took his nightstick and rained blows down on his head. Then, for good measure, she shot him three times in the head with his service revolver.

Mother and daughter managed to carry bulky Freddie downstairs and outside to a waiting wagon. They carted the dead man to a vacant lot and dumped his body into Hall's pond. Scampering back home, they tidied and cleaned up like little beavers, leaving no evidence of murder in the bedroom.

Next day, Freddie's body was found. The police had the distasteful duty of informing the widow and concerned mother-in-law of their loss. Well, folks, you should have been there. The tears flowed. Maria and Theresa wailed unto the heavens. It was quite a show.

At first the police picked up Freddie's known enemies. Like every policeman, he had a few. Speaking of policemen, the investigating officer stumbled across the fact that several of Freddie's buddies were sick. Three were in hospital, but what was even more unusual, they had all become ill after partaking of Freddie's lunch.

A search of Freddie's home uncovered a mattress in a hayloft. It had three slugs deeply imbedded in the soft material. They had been fired from Freddie's own service revolver. You didn't have to be Sherlock Holmes to figure out the rest. Soon the details of Maria's previous murder trial were brought to light. The jig was up.

In the summer of 1912 the two ladies were found guilty of murder and were sentenced to life imprisonment. During the trial Maria stated that Freddie was not a bad sort, but she would never forgive him for giving away her home-cooked meals.

A NASTY LITTLE FELLOW

As I drove into the peaceful village of Bovingdon, it was early in the morning. The dew was lifting from the rolling English countryside. I couldn't help but think of Graham Young driving up to work over these very same roads, his mind contemplating how much antimony he would administer to his fellow employees. Would Diana Smart get enough to send her home for a few days? Would Peter Buck be back today? If so, it just might be his turn for a dose.

But the Graham Young story doesn't start in this quaint English village. It begins in Honeypot Lane Maternity Hospital, North London, on Sept. 7, 1947; for that was the day Graham was born.

Molly Young didn't have an easy pregnancy. She had pleurisy while carrying Graham, and although her new son grew to be a healthy baby, it was discovered that Molly had contracted tuberculosis. She died two days before Christmas when Graham was three months old.

Fred Young, a machine setter by trade, was beside himself with grief at the loss of his wife. He decided to keep his little family as close to him as possible without the benefit of a mother. Fred had one other child, a daughter, Winnifred, who was 8-years-old at the time of her mother's death. Winnie and her father went to live with Fred's mother at Links Rd., while Graham moved in with an aunt and uncle at 768 North Circular Rd. in the Neasdon section of North London. The two addresses were not that far apart, and the little family managed to get together each weekend.

Three years later, Fred Young met another lady named Molly. At the age of 33, Fred calculated that he could still have a chance for a happy and contented life with a new wife and his two children. He married Molly, purchased the

11

house at 768 North Circular Rd., and moved in with Winnie and 3-year-old Graham.

As Graham grew up it was noted that he wasn't a joiner, or what is known as a group person. He read incessantly. Other than playing with his sister and a cousin, he kept pretty much to himself. Throughout his early years in school he was considered to be well above average in his studies. His stepmother, Molly, doted on Graham, who appeared to return her love with genuine affection.

At the age of 9 Graham Young was experimenting with varnish and nail polish. He was not doing anything malicious with these substances, but experimenting with them to ascertain the qualities inherent in various products. For a 9-year-old child, many would think this advanced element of curiosity in Graham's makeup to be a very admirable trait.

When Molly found acid and ether in Graham's room, she rightly felt that her son's interest had become abnormal for a child his age. Upon being questioned, Graham told his mother that he had found the substances in garbage thrown out by the local drugstore. Later she found books on witchcraft and the Nazi party in Graham's room.

By the time Graham was 12, his teachers believed that he had an outstanding future in the field of chemistry. Unknown to them, he was poisoning rats and performing autopsies on their bodies. His family was continually amazed at his advanced knowledge of chemicals. They could show Graham a detergent or waxing agent and he would rhyme off the chemicals which made up the product and what interaction was involved to make the substances perform as advertised.

At the age of 13 Graham knew the exact quantities of various poisons which could prove to be fatal. He also knew the effects of administering small quantities of certain poisons over a prolonged period of time. In fact, Graham was now an expert on the subject of poison. While everyone thought him a quiet little boy, no one knew the extent of his weird obsession.

In April of 1961, Graham gave a cock-and-bull story to the chemist in his neighborhood, and managed to purchase 25 grams of antimony. He signed the poison book with the fictitious name M. E. Evans, and gave a phony address. Out of his allowance received from his father, and with money from odd jobs performed at a local cafe, Graham continued to purchase quantities of antimony.

His closest school chum, Chris Williams, remembers that Graham often showed him a vial of poison. Chris thought it was a great joke, somewhat akin to the country boy showing his pet frog to his buddies.

Once the boys had a falling out, as little boys often do. A few days later Chris had severe stomach pains. He had to leave school for the day. All through the spring and summer of 1961, Chris suffered from severe stomach pains which were often accompanied by vomiting. Later he realized that his discomfort always followed those occasions when he and Graham skipped school together. On those days Graham was in the habit of sharing his sandwiches with Chris.

Chris' stomach pains and headaches became so bad that he was forced to visit his family doctor, Dr. Lancelot Wills. The doctor couldn't find anything specifically wrong with Chris, but thought his headaches were migraines.

One day, while cleaning Graham's room, Molly found a bottle of antimony. She had no idea what it was, but clearly understood the skull and crossbones on the label. She told Fred of her discovery. They both faced Graham and forbade him to have such dangerous substances in the house. Molly then went around to the chemist shop named on the bottle and, in no uncertain terms, told the chemist never to sell Graham any dangerous materials. Unknown to his parents, Graham merely changed chemists.

It wasn't long after this incident that Molly Young began to have an upset stomach. She felt weak and lethargic. She often discussed her illness with Graham. It was his custom to have tea with his mother every day after school. Finally, Molly became so ill she was taken to hospital, where she made a speedy recovery. Her illness was thought to be an ulcer. Poison was never suspected.

It is interesting to note that once antimony has passed through the body, no trace can be detected. Molly's recovery was to be temporary.

One day Winnie, now an attractive 22-year-old girl with a steady boyfriend, collapsed outside a cinema. She, too, was having periodic spells of abdominal pain accompanied by vomiting. This most recent attack set Winnie thinking. Why hadn't it occurred to her before? Her kid brother with his silly chemistry experiments. No doubt he had used some of the family dishes to perform the experiments. Some toxic substance might have adhered to a cup, causing Molly and her to become ill. She decided to speak to her father.

Fred Young didn't believe that Graham would bring poison into the house after being told to keep the terrible stuff away. Nevertheless, Fred gave Graham a real tongue lashing.

Soon Fred came down with a severe case of cramps. He never complained much, because at the same time his wife Molly became seriously ill. This time she had a complete new set of symptoms. She woke up on Easter Saturday, 1962, with a sensation of pins and needles in her hands and feet. Graham was concerned and solicitous towards his stepmother. It was decided to rush Molly to the hospital.

Once in hospital Molly said to one of the doctors, "I hope you're not going to be long about this, because I've got my husband's dinner to get." Within minutes of making this frivolous remark, Molly Young, aged 38, was dead. For about a year Graham had been feeding Molly antimony and observing the results. On the evening before Molly died, Graham had laced a trifle with twenty grains of thallium. It was this massive dose which caused her death. Graham probably didn't know it, but he had just become the first person in England ever to commit murder by the administration of deadly, tasteless, odorless thallium.

A post mortem failed to reveal the true cause of death. The following Thursday Molly was cremated. Graham Young, at the age of 14, had committed the perfect murder. When mourners gathered at the family residence to pay their respects, Graham doctored a sandwich with a small quantity of antimony. One of his mother's relatives became violently ill. Graham was just having a little fun.

A few days after his wife's funeral, Fred Young suffered a series of stomach pains accompanied by violent bouts of vomiting. Finally his daughter Winnie forced him to see their family physician, Dr. Wills. The doctor could find no reason for the illness, but was startled when, at the conclusion of the examination, Fred collapsed on the office floor. He was rushed to Willisden General Hospital, where Molly had died less than two weeks before.

After spending two days in the hospital, often comforted

by his son who visited him constantly, Fred Young began to feel better. Graham seemed to enjoy himself around the hospital, amazing doctors by his knowledge of things medical. Fred was taken home, but in a few days his pain became so severe that Winnie rushed her father back to the hospital.

That same night doctors were surprised when extensive tests confirmed that Fred was suffering from antimony poisoning.

We must pause here to keep in mind that Graham was a quiet, studious youngster of 14. It was difficult for his family to accept the facts as we are able to do from the benefit of hindsight. Graham's father was the first to actually believe that his son had been administering poison to the entire family for more than a year. Doctors told him that one more dose of antimony would have proven fatal. Fred Young recovered, but has a permanently damaged liver as a result of his son's handiwork. He also lives today with the realization that Graham was responsible for his stepmother's death.

While Fred Young lingered in hospital with his dark suspicions, direct action came from another source. Graham's chemistry teacher, Mr. Hughes, heard of Mr. Young being rushed to hospital so soon after his wife's death. Lately Mr. Hughes had wondered about Graham's lack of interest in his chemistry experiments. It appeared that the boy was obsessed with experiments using poisons, and recording data derived from his experiments in a notebook. Mr. Hughes decided to stay late at school and search Graham's desk. He found several bottles of poison.

Recalling Chris Williams' illness, Mr. Hughes felt the whole thing was just too much. He contacted the headmaster of the school and together they went to see Dr. Wills. The three men exchanged notes and, for the first time, the magnitude of Graham's poisonous endeavors came to light.

They arranged for a psychiatrist, posing as a child guidance counsellor, to consult with Graham. Graham loved to display his knowledge of pharmacology and had a learned discussion with the psychiatrist, who was amazed at the lad's knowledge. He went straight to the police with his suspicions.

Next day Detective Inspector Edward Crabbe searched Graham's room. He found quantities of antimony, thallium, digitalis, ionine, atropine, and barium chloride. When Graham was searched, police found a vial of antimony, as well as two bottles of thallium, in his shirt. Later he referred to the vial of antimony as his little friend. Taken to jail the following morning, Graham revealed his entire career as a poisoner to the police.

Graham Young was unique. Obviously his age alone set him apart from most killers, but above all the fact that he lacked any motive made his crimes different. He did not dislike the people he poisoned. They were given poison specifically because they were close at hand and could be observed. Graham was experimenting, much as a scientist does with guinea pigs.

On July 5, 1962, Graham was tried in London's Old Bailey, one of the youngest ever to appear in the famous old court. He was charged with poisoning his father, his sister, and his schoolchum, Chris Williams. The charge of murdering his stepmother was not pressed. Her ashes had been scattered, and it was believed nothing could be gained by bringing further charges against such a young boy.

Dr. Christopher Fysh, a psychiatrist attached to the Ashford Remand Centre, where Graham had been housed awaiting his trial, told of his conclusions after having extensive conversations with Graham. He quoted Graham as telling him, "I am missing my antimony. I am missing the power it gives me." The doctor elaborated on Graham's knowledge of drugs, and stated that on several occasions Graham had corrected him in minor areas when the properties of various drugs were discussed. Dr. Fysh suggested that Graham was obsessed with the sense of power his poisons gave him. In the doctor's opinion, given the chance, Graham would continue to experiment on humans. Dr. Fysh thought Graham should be confined to a maximum security hospital. As a result, he was sentenced to Broadmoor for a period of 15 years.

In July, 1962, the gates of the ominous old brick structure closed behind 14-year-old Graham Young. He was one of the youngest patients ever to be admitted, but not the youngest. That distinction belonged to Bill Giles, who died there at the age of 87. He had been convicted of setting fire to a hayrick at the age of 10 in 1885. Giles had spent 77 years in Broadmoor, and coincidentally died three months before Graham was admitted.

About a month after Graham arrived at Broadmoor, an incident occurred which, all things considered, gives one room for thought.

John Berridge was a 23-year-old patient who had killed his parents. Quite suddenly one day he went into convulsions, collapsed and died. A post mortem revealed that his death was due to cyanide poisoning. The inquiry which followed established that no cyanide was kept at Broadmoor. However, the investigation also revealed that laurel bushes, from which an expert could extract cyanide, grew adjacent to the institution.

Several patients immediately confessed to poisoning Berridge. Among those confessing was Graham Young. He was the only one who could explain in detail the processes involved in extracting cyanide from laurel bushes. The authorities chose not to believe any of the confessions. They leaned towards the theory that somehow the poison was smuggled into the institution. The Berridge case remains unsolved to this day.

At first Graham Young, the lad from the respectable suburb of North London, had difficulty adjusting to the maximum security institution, but as the years went by he seemed to respond to psychiatric treatment. Dr. Edgar Udwin held high hopes for a complete recovery and early release for his young patient.

Meanwhile, Graham's family regarded his poisonous ways as a mental illness. His sister Winnie, cousins, aunts, and uncles all felt that Graham had been sick and was now on the road to recovery. His father Fred had a difficult time accepting this live and let live view. He could forgive Graham for almost everything, but he could never forget that his own son had studied and apparently enjoyed the death of his poor wife Molly.

After consulting with Graham's sister Winnie, it was decided by Dr. Udwin that Graham be released for one week in November, 1970. In the eight years of Graham's incarceration at Broadmoor, Winnie had married and was now the mother of a baby girl. She and her husband decided, in conjunction with Dr. Udwin, that no precautions against poison be taken during the week of Graham's visit.

Winnie now lived in a fashionable suburb of Hemel Hempstead, a city of 85,000, located about 30 miles north of

London. Graham visited for the week, and the experiment was a huge success. With his doctor's consent and his family's urging, he visited at Christmastime for another week and was a delight to have in the house.

On Feb. 4, 1971, Graham, at the age of 23, was released from Broadmoor. He was sent directly to Slough, to the government resettlement centre for 13 weeks training as a stock keeper and shipper.

Nearing the completion of his course, on April 24, 1971, Graham performed two tasks which were to have far reaching effects. He applied for a job as store keeper at John Hadland Photographic Instrumentation Ltd., Bovingdon, Hertsfordshire. Then he went to the centre of London, walked into a drugstore, and purchased 25 grams of antimony.

It was a stroke of luck when Graham's application for employment was accepted at Hadland's in Bovingdon, a quaint rural village only three miles from Hemel Hempstead.

Graham would have the steadying influence of a member of his family, but would still live and work in an independent environment. He took a room at 20 Maynards Rd. in Hemel Hempstead. His landlord, Mohammed Saddiq, a native of Pakistan, had no idea a murderer and former inmate of Broadmoor was his new roomer. At the time Mr. Saddiq didn't speak one word of English.

Seven years later, when I knocked on the door of 29 Maynards Rd., Mr. Saddiq well remembered his infamous tenant. He led me up the stairs to the room Graham had occupied. He pointed out the windowsill where Graham had stocked enough poison to kill scores of people. There, in a corner, was the bed under which Graham kept his diary of death. Mr. Saddiq assured me that his star roomer never ate at his home, nor had he ever entered his kitchen. Seven years before, Mr. Saddiq had considered himself fortunate to have such a quiet, well behaved roomer in his home.

I drove the three miles to the village of Bovingdon, and met with a director of Hadland's, Terry Johnson. Mr. Johnson explained how Graham Young became an employee of the firm. Young answered an advertisement and was granted an interview. He was highly recommended by the training school, having just completed a course in storekeeping, the exact position the firm was attempting to fill.

He accounted for the previous nine years by telling Mr. Foster of Hadland's that he'd had a nervous breakdown upon the death of his mother, but was now completely cured. Before hiring Graham, Mr. Foster checked out his story.

The government training centre got in touch with Dr. Udwin, the psychiatrist who was instrumental in securing Graham's release from Broadmoor. He obligingly sent along a letter confirming that Young was normal and competent in every way. At no time was Hadland's informed that Young had been a patient at Broadmoor, or had been convicted of being a poisoner.

On May 10, 1971, Graham went to work. He became assistant storekeeper at a salary of 24 pounds a week. The one hundred employees at Hadland's are a friendly cheerful group. Mr. Johnson, who showed me the premises, was called Terry by everyone we met. Hadland's exports expensive industrial photographic equipment all over the world. The firm received some measure of satisfaction from its mention in Guinness Book of World Records. They have produced a camera which takes 600 million pictures a second.

The men in the storeroom welcomed Graham in his new position. Within days he had gained the reputation of being a bit quiet, but certainly a nice enough bloke. His boss, Bob Egle, was 59-years-old and looking forward to retirement. Bob had been married for 39 years. He found out that his new assistant Graham loved to hear of his wartime experiences, especially his evacuation from Dunkirk.

Fred Biggs was 60 and the senior employee in the Works in Progress Department. The two older men liked Graham Young.

Jethro Batt worked side-by-side with Graham in the stores. Each day after work Jethro would give Graham a lift the three miles back to Hemel Hempstead.

Twice a day May Bartlett wheeled a tea wagon down the long hall to the stores area. Members of the staff would then fetch their tea from the wagon. That is, before Graham came to work at Hadland's. Soon it became customary for Graham to pick up the tea from the wagon and distribute it to his fellow employees in the stores.

About a month after Graham started working at Hadland's, his boss Bob Egle became ill. He took a few days off work, but the pains in his stomach persisted. On June 18, he and his wife took a week's vacation at Great Yarmouth. The time off seemed to work wonders. Bob appeared so much better when he returned.

Two days before Bob was due back, Graham had travelled to London and purchased 25 grams of thallium. Within 24 hours of stating that he was feeling just great again after his vacation, Bob Egle took terribly ill at work. He went home, complaining of numbness in his fingers. Later he began to stagger. By morning the weight of the sheets on his bed caused him excruciating pain.

On successive days Bob Egle was transferred from West Herts Hospital in Hemel Hempstead to the intensive care unit at St. Albans City Hospital. He lingered in great pain for eight days before dying.

Back at Hadland's, everyone was concerned about the well-liked boss of the stores passing away so suddenly. None seemed to take it any harder than the new man, Graham Young.

A post mortem was performed on Bob Egle. Death was attributed to bronco-pneumonia in conjunction with poly-neuritis. The following Monday, several members of the staff indicated a desire to attend Egle's funeral. It was decided that the managing director, Mr. Geoffrey Foster would attend representing management, while Graham Young would represent the staff. The two men travelled together to the funeral. Foster remembers being surprised at Young's inti-mate knowledge of the medical diagnosis surrounding Egle's death.

Diana Smart, a fill-in employee in the stores section at Hadland's, didn't feel well all that summer. Nothing severe, but she was in enough discomfort to force her to go home several days during that July and August.

In September, Peter Buck, the import export manager, noticed that he always felt queasy after tea time. A few weeks later Diana Smart's attacks became more severe. Around this time Jethro Batt also became ill. One day he accepted a cup of tea from Graham and then gave him a lift to Hemel Hempstead. Next day Batt couldn't raise himself out of bed. Pains racked his stomach and chest. In the ensu-ing days his hair began to fall out in large tufts. He suffered hallucinations and became so distressed that he wanted to kill himself. Batt was admitted to hospital. Unknown to him or his doctors, the fact that he was removed from Graham Young and his poisonous ways saved his life. He gradually recovered.

In the meantime David Tilson experienced violent stomach pains accompanied by vomiting. He was rushed to St. Albans Hospital, where he too started to lose his hair. After a short while, he began to recover and was discharged.

It seemed that everyone at Hadland's was taking ill. By now the death of Bob Egle had the entire staff on edge. Could the outbreak of the strange undiagnosed illness be the same thing that killed Bob?

On a weekend early in November, the stores department at Hadland's was sorely understaffed. Bob Egle was dead. Both Tilson and Batt were off sick. Fred Biggs and his wife came in on a weekend to help Graham Young catch up. Graham made tea that Saturday for Biggs. Next morning Fred could hardly move. He would never return to work. Twenty days later Fred Biggs was dead.

By now, as one can well imagine, rumors were running rampant through the Hadland plant. For some time previous to the current outbreak of sickness in the area, a virus had on occasion swept through Bovingdon, causing stomach complaints. These outbreaks were often blamed on the Bovingdon Bug.

To quell the rumors and suspicions of the employees, the management of Hadland's decided to call in Dr. Robert Hynd, Medical Officer of Health for the Hemel Hempstead area. Dr. Hynd inspected the plant and could find no cause for the wave of illness. Despite the doctor's statement that the cause of the illness didn't originate in the plant, rumors still persisted. They ranged from toxic chemicals being used in the manufacturing processes to medieval curses. After Fred Biggs died, some men even considered leaving Hadland's.

Management took another stab at coming up with the solution to the riddle. They called in the local general practitioner, Dr. Iain Anderson, to have an informal, morale boosting chat with the employees.

Everyone gathered in the cafeteria to hear Dr. Anderson. He explained that the authorities had ruled out radiation.

They also checked out thallium, which was sometimes used in the manufacture of index lenses such as those manufactured at Hadland's. However, Hadland's did not keep thallium on the premises, so this agent had been dismissed as a possible cause of the sickness. The doctor leaned heavily toward a particularly strong strain of the Bovingdon Bug as being at the bottom of all the trouble. He assured the employees that the authorities were doing everything possible to isolate the cause of the dreadful sickness.

At the conclusion of his talk, the doctor inquired if there were any questions. Dr. Anderson was amazed when one employee, Graham Young, posed complicated questions regarding heavy metal poisoning and its effects. The doctor had a hard time getting the young man to sit down. The meeting was hastily brought to a close.

Dr. Anderson later made it a point to find Young and pursue the subject of poison. Again, he was dumbfounded at Young's detailed knowledge. Who was Graham Young, anyhow? Dr. Anderson and the chairman of the board, John Hadland, discussed the matter. Hadland called in the authorities, who checked Young's record at Scotland Yard. It revealed that he had been released just six months earlier from Broadmoor, where he had been sentenced for poisoning.

In Graham's room at 29 Maynards Rd. police uncovered his diary, detailing the dates and quantities of poison he had administered to Hadland employees. Graham Young had been playing God. He chose that some should die, while others should live. All were observed during their illness.

Young confessed to all his crimes, and to this day has never shown any remorse for the suffering he caused. All tests and examinations have indicated that he has above average intelligence, and is, in the legal sense, perfectly sane.

Young received several sentences of life imprisonment for his crimes. His victims, some of whom still live and work in the Hemel Hempstead area, want to forget Graham Young.

As I prepared to leave the Hadland plant with its airy, cheery atmosphere, I asked director Terry Johnson, who had lived through the terror which was Graham Young, how in a sentence he would describe what went on there.

He answered without hesitation, "It was unbelievable."

VENOM MARKED POLICY PAID

There have been some strange and fascinating murder weapons employed by men and women intent on hastening their victims' demise. We have run the gauntlet from conventional baseball bats and bullets, to more bizarre rare poisons and simulated accidents. You may think that we have explored every method used to commit the dastardly act of murder, but—would you believe a rattlesnake?

Bob James was born in Alabama around 1921 to dirt poor cotton farmers. He finished a couple of years of formal education before his brother-in-law, who was a barber, sent him to a barber school in Birmingham. Young Bob learned a trade and, for a while, worked at a part-time job. For all intents and purposes he promised to become a law abiding, hardworking citizen.

Then one day he just took off without telling a soul. For years he drifted across the U.S., working at odd jobs. Bob James was one of those men who was always trying to impress the ladies. He became pretty good at it. He perfected his natural Southern drawl to go with a practised line, and had no trouble finding female companionship.

Bob wasn't that bad to look at either. He had wavy red hair, delicate, even features, and was of average build and height. Altogether, not an unattractive man.

Bob's mother passed away, leaving her only boy a few hundred dollars insurance money. Son of a gun, Bob thought, what an easy way to get cash if the need ever arose. In the meantime, he gravitated to Los Angeles, California, where, in 1931, he opened a high class barbershop. The shop did well, at least well enough to provide Bob with the means to wine and dine his lady friends.

In 1932 he married Winona Wallace. Winsome Winona

was no sooner Mrs. James than Bob suggested she take out a few insurance policies on her life. Naturally her ever-lovin' husband was the beneficiary. Within two months of her marriage Winona had a total of $14,000 insurance, payable to Bob should she meet her death accidentally.

A short while later Bob and Winona took a vacation, sort of a belated honeymoon. The vacation was interrupted near Pike's Peak, Colorado, when unfortunately, their car went over a cliff. Lady Luck had smiled upon Bob. He had been able to jump clear of the plunging car and run for help. When he brought some men back to the scene of the accident, he almost fainted when he discovered the car hadn't plunged all the way down the cliff. About 100 feet down the hill a huge boulder had stopped the vehicle. Miraculously, Winona was alive. Rushed to a hospital in Colorado Springs, she recovered, but could remember nothing of the details of the accident.

When Winona was released from the hospital, thoughtful Bob rented a lonely cabin near Manitou so that his wife would be able to rest quietly while she regained her health. Bob later mentioned to acquaintances that he was concerned about Winona. She seemed to be suffering from dizzy spells.

It wasn't long after voicing his concern that Bob, accompanied by a young boy helping him carry groceries, found Winona's body in the bathtub. There she was, lying on her back, with her feet dangling over the end of the tub. Death was obviously due to drowning. Winona was ultimately sent to her final resting place without any official inquiry ever being made into her death.

Bob collected the fourteen big ones without even a murmur of suspicion from the insurance companies. Now loaded with cash, he went on a buying spree, purchasing clothing, luggage, and a shiny new Pierce Arrow convertible.

To settle his nerves about his great loss, Bob took a trip back home to Birmingham. Remember his brother-in-law, the barber? Well, wouldn't you know it; he had a robust, healthy 18-year-old daughter, pretty as a picture and twice as willing. Bob fell hard for his niece, Lois.

When Bob left Birmingham Lois was there, cuddled up beside him in the convertible. Once back in L.A., he enrolled Lois in a school where she learned to become a manicurist. She also worked part time in his barbershop.

But Bob couldn't change the habits of a lifetime. Soon he was cavorting with several other ladies and, in a moment of weakness, married one. As soon as the nuptials were officially consummated, Bob couldn't stand the new wife. He immediately instituted proceedings to have the marriage annulled.

On the rebound he became involved with another manicurist in his shop. Mary Busch couldn't wait to marry Bob. In fact, she insisted on having the marriage ceremony performed before Bob's previous marriage was officially annulled. Bob, cunning devil that he was, got a friend to pose as a minister and perform a phony ceremony. Mary thought she had really tied the knot. Bob, of course, was the beneficiary on the $10,000 worth of insurance policies taken out on Mary's life.

During the summer of 1935 Bob and Mary lived in apparent happiness in a small bungalow at the foot of the Sierra Madre mountains. It was a romantic but lonely spot, just perfect for what Bob had in mind.

In June, Jim Hope, a drifter, walked into Bob's barbershop looking for work. He was made to order for the scheme Bob was hatching. Bob told Hope that he would pay him $100 if he could get him a rattlesnake. Hope at first thought the proposition a bit strange but $100 was big money back in 1935. He managed to purchase one from a snake dealer for $6. Bob placed a chicken in the rattler's cage. When he looked in the following morning, the chicken was dead. He knew then he had a murder weapon in his possession.

By informing Bob that she was pregnant, Mary gave him the opportunity he needed. He convinced her that she should have an abortion. In preparation for the abortion, gullible Mary followed Bob's instructions to the letter. On Aug. 4, 1935 Bob persuaded Mary to let herself be strapped to the kitchen table. She was then blindfolded and a strip of adhesive tape placed over her mouth. Bob brought his cage containing the rattlesnake into the house. He opened the sliding glass side of the reptile's cage and placed Mary's foot inside. The snake struck. The box was taken away and later destroyed by Hope. He sold the snake that same day.

Later Mary's leg swelled and she began to suffer excruciating pain. That evening Bob and Hope drank whiskey waiting for Mary to die. Despite the pain, the stricken woman continued to live. In desperation Bob filled the bathtub with water and drowned his wife. The dead woman was then carried outside, where the upper portion of her body was placed in a fishpond in the yard.

A friend found Mary's body. She had apparently suffered a dizzy spell and fallen into the pond. The local coroner stated that the cause of death was due to an accident. The insurance companies balked, and Bob had to settle for $3,500 on his total claims of $10,000.

Bob had apparently succeeded again. Six months went by before a liquor store proprietor called on his lawyer with a strange story. He told how the previous summer a man named Hope had come into his store in an agitated state inquiring where he could buy a rattlesnake. He had mumbled something about planning to murder a woman. The liquor store owner had thought about it for some time. He decided that since a woman had died under suspicious circumstances he had better tell the story.

Soon the police were on the trail of the rattlesnake purchase, and the whole story started to fit together. Hope was apprehended. To save his skin, he confessed to the police. Bob then confessed, giving a slightly different version, in order to implicate Hope.

Now that Mary's death had turned into a murder case, the authorities decided to look into the circumstances surrounding Winona's death. They came up with a man who had visited the scene of the car accident at Pike's Point. Now that they asked, he had always wondered how a man could leap from a runaway car and not even get a wrinkle in his suit. The investigating officers knew they had a double killer on their hands.

Because of the weird rattlesnake angle, the murder trials of Jim Hope and Bob James received national coverage. Hope was found guilty of murder in the first degree and sentenced to life imprisonment. Bob James was also found guilty of murder in the first degree. After many appeals he was hanged. James was the last man to hang in California. The state introduced the gas chamber a short time later.

THIS TIME ANNA LOST HER HEAD

It has been necessary to turn over many a yellowed document to reveal the diabolical life of Anna Zwanziger. But Anna is worth every cobweb, so let's start at the very beginning.

Herr Schonleben, a fat, jolly man, ran a successful saloon in Nuremberg, Germany. One day in 1760 a young lad burst into Herr Schonleben's watering hole and informed the jolly German that Frau Schonleben had just given birth to a lovely little girl. The lovely little girl was to later be remembered as a lovely little monster. Her name was Anna.

As the years passed Herr Schonleben often reflected while down at the saloon dispensing suds that his teenage daughter was not a raving beauty. She had rather thin lips and a decidedly too thin nose. Dark brown eyes stared out of sockets which appeared to be set much too far into her head. The overall mousey appearance was not enhanced by a somewhat sallow complexion. No, you definitely had to say Anna was not a looker.

Anna's daddy, kept a sharp and alert eye out for unsuspecting potential husbands. That's how Herr Zwanziger got into the act. Hearing of the generous dowry which would accompany Anna en route to the altar, Herr Zwanziger, a struggling attorney, paid her a call. Anna, overcome by her newfound popularity, was thrilled by the dashing attorney. It wasn't long before Fraulein Schonleben became Frau Zwanziger.

After the nuptials it was only a matter of days before Anna found out that Zwanziger's main occupation was not the law, but a passion for good friends and alcoholic beverage. Year after year, Zwanziger drank his days and nights away until he had gone through Anna's money and his liver.

Herr Zwanziger was laid to rest after the proper complimentary eulogies had been expressed by those who knew he was a good for nothing.

Zwanziger left our Anna with a host of bad memories and bad debts. She was now faced with the very real task of making a living. She tried many avenues to support herself, but was singularly unsuccessful at all of them. For a while she operated a confectionery business. It failed. She tried selling toys and cooking for a shospital. She even travelled with a circus, but hated the transient life.

The years swiftly flew by, as they have a habit of doing. Anna, now in her late 40s, was driven to perform her first dishonest act. She stole a ring from a neighbor's house and got away with it. When she sold the valuable ring, she received enough money to keep her going for several months. This crime business, thought Anna, is not half bad. Besides providing the necessities of life, it gave her a precarious thrill. Anna moved to the little town of Pegnitz to gather her wits.

. At this time Anna became obsessed with the idea that she had no one to take care of her in her approaching old age. Someway, somehow, she must become affluent enough to take care of the problem herself.

As luck would have it, while these dire thoughts were dancing through her head, she learned of a judge named Glaser, who was separated from his wife. Glaser was looking for a housekeeper. Anna applied for the job, was interviewed, and was accepted for the position.

It is believed that Anna hatched her little scheme before she left Glaser's office. It was as simple as all get out. She would become Frau Glaser. Of course, there was the present Frau Glaser to be dealt with before this new thought of Anna's could become a reality.

Cunning Anna decided first things first. She had to somehow lure Frau Glaser back to her hubby's bed. She set about accomplishing her devious ends by sending little notes to the estranged wife pointing out how the judge longed for her company. Soon Frau Glaser was replying to the concerned and considerate housekeeper that she too longed to be reinstated in the judge's comfortable big home. Once given the opening, it didn't take Anna long to effect a reconciliation.

and, at the same time, ingratiate herself with both Frau and Herr Glaser.

One thing you had to say about Anna; she did things with a flourish. Frau Glaser's homecoming was accompanied by large bouquets of flowers strategically placed around the house. Anna even hired a local orchestra for the happy reunion. The whole thing went off smashingly. Frau Glaser walked into the front door of her home and into the arms of her husband.

Within days Frau Glaser was suffering from severe stomach pains. It was no wonder either. Anna had given her three massive doses of arsenic. The housekeeper was apparently beside herself at this tragic turn of events. Her grief was almost uncontrollable when Frau Glaser died in agony.

After the funeral, which was interrupted on several occasions by wails of sorrow from Anna, our heroine decided to get down to business. It was time to turn on the charm and become the new Frau Glaser.

Alas, the best laid plans of mice and men often go astray, especially in the murder business. Herr Glaser showed a decided tendency to be left alone during his period of mourning. In fact, he became something of a recluse. Within a matter of days after the funeral Anna was shattered when she was informed that her services were no longer required.

It had all been for naught, but what the heck, now that she had perfected a murder method there had to be other fish ready for frying. Sure enough Anna came up with another judge.

Herr Grohmann was a middle aged, wealthy gentleman who lived in Sanspareil. He suffered from gout. Anna became his housekeeper, but the setup wasn't exactly perfect. Grohmann had a young, attractive girlfriend whom he planned to marry. We'll see about that, Anna thought to herself. She turned on the charm, but Grohmann wasn't susceptible to sex in an unattractive package when he was already sampling the real thing with his betrothed.

Anna didn't have a chance. All her anger was directed at Grohmann himself. She dipped into her rather ample packet of arsenic and gave Grohmann a suitable dose in his chicken soup. He was dead three hours later.

Anna once again found a post as housekeeper in the home

of a member of the legal profession. Herr Gebhard was a prosperous, overweight magistrate. His wife was a nag, and very, very pregnant.

Now fun's fun, but her two previous murders had brought Anna no material gain. She figured three times lucky. Things would be different this time around. Anna set about feeding arsenic to Frau Gebhard. During her mistress' inevitable illness Anna nursed her night and day. She was so devoted she wouldn't allow anyone else to feed her patient. Despite the loving care Frau Gebhard became weaker and weaker. Just before she was about to give up the ghost, clever Anna called in a doctor. The medic noted that his patient was beyond help. His diagnosis proved to be extremely accurate. Frau Gebhard died two hours after he examined her.

Anna took care of the funeral arrangements. Everything was going along just swell. Soon Gebhard would grow tired of mourning for his dearly departed spouse, and lo and behold, he would discover sweet considerate Anna.

Darn the luck. Would you believe that one of the servant girls in the house was a gorgeous well endowed fraulein. Rightly or wrongly, it seemed to Anna that Gebhard was paying far too much attention to her. Anna slipped her just enough arsenic to take her out of contention for a few weeks.

Again the path seemed clear for Anna to take the romantic initiative. This time it was Gebhard himself who spoiled everything. To end his period of mourning, he decided to throw a huge dinner party. Anna hated the idea of young, good looking frauleins twittering about trying to get their tentacles into what was rightfully hers. Try as she might, she couldn't talk her master out of his party.

That's when she lost her cool. If Gebhard wanted to throw a dinner party, she would prepare one he would never forget. Anna laced all the food with arsenic. Everyone except Gebhard became frightfully sick right at the dinner table. The other servants in the house, many of whom knew Anna wanted Gebhard for herself, thought the whole thing so funny they made the mistake of laughing right in front of the housekeeper.

That same evening they too came down with severe cramps after partaking of supper. Neither guests nor servants died from Anna's little treats, but the servants suspected the truth. They went to Gebhard and insisted that the remainder of their meal be examined. A chemist informed him that the food had been laced with arsenic.

Anna was dismissed immediately. The next day Gebhard, figuring that he had been too lenient with his housekeeper, informed the police of his suspicions.

Anna was traced to her hometown of Nuremburg, where she was arrested and charged with murder. She maintained her innocence throughout her trial. When she was found guilty, she collapsed in court. Later, awaiting her execution, she wrote a long confession in which she admitted her murderous ways.

Anna was executed by the sword, when she was decapitated in July, 1811.

WICKED DOCTOR CREAM

The 1920's have often been referred to as the golden age of sport. Babe Ruth was clouting home runs, while Jack Dempsey was clouting anyone who stood in his way.

In the murder business the period between 1880 and 1895 should be called the golden age of mayhem. It gave rise to so many unusual murders. A chap known as Jack the Ripper, who was never positively identified, but who lives on in infamy, was roaming the streets of London cutting up ladies of the night. On this side of the big pond a God-fearing, church going New England lady named Lizzie Borden was accused of chopping up her Mummie and Daddy with a hatchet.

With the murder stage being so crowded with nefarious players, it is no wonder that Dr. Neill Cream never gained the notoriety he so richly deserved.

Neill first saw the light of day in Glasgow, Scotland in 1850. His family migrated to Canada when he was five. Nothing is known of his formative years other than that he applied himself diligently to his schoolwork and did exceedingly well throughout high school. He continued on to McGill University in Montreal, where he received his medical degree. He later took post graduate work in London and Edinburgh before returning to Canada.

For the next five years Neill Cream led an eventful, if somewhat jaded, existence. He set up practice in various Canadian towns and cities, but was always forced to stay on the move. You see, Dr. Cream's medical standards were decidedly below the norm, particularly when he was examining female patients. In fact, it wasn't an uncommon sight to see a lady running out of Dr. Cream's office in a state of undress. Finally, he found the temperature so unbearably hot that he left Canada for Chicago, in order to have more freedom to practise his particular brand of medicine.

In 1881 Dr. Cream went too far. He gave a huge quantity of strychnine to a patient named Stott. It is believed that the motive was twofold. Stott had a pretty wife whom the doctor was examining all the time, although her neighbors later stated that this was very strange since she was never sick a day in her life. It is believed to this day that Mrs. Stott was involved with Cream in her husband's sudden demise. At the time of Stott's death, Cream was trying to place a large insurance policy on the unfortunate man's life, with himself as the beneficiary.

Stott's death at first was attributed to natural causes. Then Dr. Cream did an extraordinary thing, which he continued to do throughout his criminal career. He started writing letters. He wrote to both the coroner and the district attorney suggesting that Stott's body be exhumed. Finally, at the anonymous urging of Cream the body was disinterred. Upon examination, it was found to be chock full of strychnine.

Dr. Cream and Mrs. Stott took off, but were soon apprehended and indicted for murder. Mrs. Stott, cutie that she was, testified for the state. Charges against her were dropped. Dr. Cream was found guilty of second degree murder and was sentenced to life imprisonment. In 1881 the prison gates of Joliet closed behind the strange doctor, but his career was far from over. In 1891, after Cream had spent just under 10 years in prison, Gov. Fifer of Illinois commuted his sentence, and Neill Cream walked out of prison, a free man. The governor had made a horrendous error.

While he had been serving time in prison, Cream's father died, leaving him an inheritance of $16,000, a veritable fortune before the turn of the century. Dr. Cream picked up the cash and headed for England, arriving in London on Oct. 1, 1891. Whether it was the London fog or whatever, Dr. Cream didn't waste any time pursuing his secondary occupation, that of poisoner.

A 19-year-old prostitute, Ellen Donworth, let herself be picked up by Cream. During the course of the evening her tall, austere looking friend, sporting a top hat, offered her a drink out of his flask. She took two long drags on the bottle and almost immediately began to suffer from convulsions. Her friend was nowhere to be found, but neighbors called a doctor who rushed the girl to the hospital. She died en route. An autopsy revealed that Ellen had died of strychnine poisoning.

The police had no clues to the poisoner's identity, but never fear. Our doctor Cream made sure that he received some of the recognition he craved. He wrote to the coroner offering to reveal the killer's identity in return for 200,000 pounds. The letter was signed A. O'Brien. The coroner tried to set up a rendezvous, but O'Brien-Cream never showed up.

One week after the Donworth murder another prostitute, Matilda Clover, was found in her room writhing in agony. Her client for the evening, a man who called himself Fred, had given her some pills. Before she died, she described Fred to a friend who lived in the same house. Fred was a tall, well-built man, who dressed in a cape and tall silk hat. For some reason, Matilda's death was thought to have been caused by alcoholism, but Cream would have none of it. He dashed off a note to a distinguished doctor, accusing him of poisoning Matilda with strychnine. The doctor took the letter to the police. Other distinguished people received letters accusing them of poisoning Matilda. Because of the veritable shower of letters, Matilda's body was exhumed. The cause of her death was attributed to strychnine. Scotland Yard now realized that a systematic killer was on the loose in London.

The winter months drifted by without any further murders at the hands of the mysterious poisoner with an abnormal urge for revealing his crimes in letters. Later, when every move Cream made was reviewed, the reason he stopped poisoning prostitutes during the winter months became clear. He had taken a trip to Canada, where strangely enough, he had printed 500 circulars, a copy of which follows:

ELLEN DONWORTH'S DEATH

To the Guests of the Metropole Hotel. Ladies and Gentlemen:

I hereby notify you that the person who poisoned Ellen Donworth on the 13th last October is today in the employ of the Metropole Hotel and that your lives are in danger as long as you remain in this Hotel.

London April 1892.
                                                 Yours respectfully,
                                                   W. H. Murray.

Dr. Cream never used the printed circulars, and no one knows to this day why he had them printed. They do serve to reveal Cream's perverted obsession with publicity of any kind.

With the coming of Spring, and with Cream back in England, things started to percolate once again.

Emma Shrivell, an 18-year-old prostitute and her friend, Alice March, lived in a furnished flat near Waterloo Road. In the middle of the night their screams woke the landlady. Both girls were in great pain and were convulsing violently. During brief periods when their agony subsided, they told of having a distinguished gentleman as a supper guest earlier that evening. The gentleman wore a tall tophat, called himself Fred, and claimed he was a doctor. The girls let him talk them into taking some pills. Alice March died before reaching the hospital, while Emma Shrivell lingered for five hours before she too died.

Quite by chance a bobby walking his beat had seen the two girls let their guest out into the night. He was able to provide a full description. The publicity surrounding these two deaths brought forth other ladies who had managed to escape the clutches of the mysterious Fred.

Lou Harvey told of pretending to take the pills, but unknown to Fred she had thrown them away. Violet Beverley refused a drink offered to her by the obliging Fred. Both of these ladies gave detailed descriptions of their weird acquaintance to the police.

Then Dr. Cream, still craving notoriety, did the ultimate. He complained to Scotland Yard. Using the name Dr. Neill, he told them that the police were following him and harrassing him with accusations that he was the killer of March and Shrivell. Neill told the Yard that he had nothing whatever to do with the crimes, claiming that a Dr. Harper was the real culprit.

It is difficult to understand exactly why Dr. Cream would furnish the police with information which would lead them to his doorstep. It wasn't long before the authorities discovered that Dr. Neill was really Dr. Cream. Several of the surviving ladies identified him as the elusive Fred. So did the bobby who had seen him leave March and Shrivell's flat the night they died.

Dr. Cream was 42-years-old when he was adjudged to be legally sane and placed on trial for murder. On Nov. 15, 1892 he was hanged for his crimes.

With death only seconds away Cream's sense of the dramatic was not to be denied. As the trap door sprung open he yelled, "I am Jack the R -----." Reporters ran to their files, only to find out that Dr. Cream had been securely locked up in Joliet when Jack was operating in London.

Dr. Cream suffered his greatest indignity when more than 80 years after his execution, Madame Tussaud's wax museum in London announced they were removing his wax image from their chamber of horrors. It seems there was a decided lack of interest, and anyway he wasn't scary enough.

A SWEET CASE OF MURDER BY POISON

To perform murder in Victorian England and have the case still considered to be a classic is no mean feat. In those days young people often died due to maladies caused by unsanitary conditions, contaminated water, and tainted food. Those who didn't die of natural causes were often eased into oblivion with the help of some poison or other which was not readily detected. An innovative approach was required to stand out in such a crowd.

Dr. George Lamson was such a trail blazer. At the age of 20 he was studying medicine in Paris. In 1878, by the time he was 28, he was practising medicine in London, England, and had taken a wife.

Pretty Kate John was everything a Victorian wife should have been—pleasant, gracious, devoted, and loyal to her handsome, educated husband. Kate's younger brother, Hubert, died of natural causes a year after the couple's marriage. This tragedy did have a silver lining. Hubert left the Lamsons an amount of money which enabled the good doctor to purchase a medical practice in Bournemouth.

Kate had another brother, Percy. Sixteen-year-old Percy had curvature of the spine, which left him paralyzed from the waist down. Confined to a wheel chair, he was placed in a private school, Blenheim House in Wimbledon, where he seemed to fit in well with the other boys.

All went well for some time. Being a doctor, and husband to a woman who deeply cared for her afflicted brother, it was only natural that Dr. Lamson displayed a certain concern for Percy. On Dec. 3, 1881, he visited Blenheim House.

The principal of the school, William Bedbrook, fetched Percy when the doctor arrived. Dr. Lamson had brought some treats. From a black bag he extradited some hard fruit

37

candy and a fruitcake. The doctor cut the cake with a pen-
knife, offering a slice to Percy and the principal, as well as
taking a slice himself. All three almost finished the cake at
the one sitting.

During the course of idle conversation Dr. Lamson mentioned that he had recently returned from America and had
brought back something new—gelatine capsules. The gelatine
dissolved after the capsule was swallowed, effectively doing
away with the disagreeable taste of some medicines. Both the
principal and Percy tried one. The principal's was empty, but
Percy's was filled with sugar from a sugar bowl sitting on a
table nearby. He swallowed it without tasting the sugar at
all.

The doctor terminated his visit and left the school, informing the principal that he had to catch a train later that night
for Florence.

That evening Percy complained of heartburn and went to
bed. Later he began to vomit and convulse violently. Two
doctors were summoned, but they could do nothing for the
boy. At 11:20 that same evening Percy died.

On Dec. 6 a post mortem was held, and it was the opinion
of the doctors that Percy had been poisoned. Dr. Lamson
was located in Paris. Once informed of the death in the
family he immediately returned to London. By that time the
story of his visit to the school was known to the authorities.
He was arrested and charged with murder.

On March 8, 1882, Lamson's murder trial began in London's Old Bailey. The prosecution quickly established that
Percy had been done in by aconite, one of the most lethal
poisons known to man. Dr. Lamson had purchased aconite
shortly before his visit to the school. He also was deeply in
debt and stood to gain financially from Percy's death.

In all murder cases involving poison the prosecution must
establish that the victim was in fact poisoned, and that the
accused administered the poison. It was this second point
that proved to be a sticky wicket. Bedbrook, the principal,
was present at all times during Lamson's visit. The hard
candies weren't touched. All three ate the cake. The sugar,
which went into the capsule consumed by Percy, came from
the school's own sugar bowl.

Despite this little problem, and the doctor's insistence
throughout that he was innocent, he was found guilty and

sentenced to hang. The sentence was carried out on April 28, 1882. The day before he was hanged Dr. Lamson confessed in writing to the murder of his brother-in-law. He never did state how he had administered the poison, and the solution to the case has baffled criminologists down through the years.

Here is the diabolical method most accepted by those who have closely studied the case. The speculation is that the doctor injected aconite into a raisin, which he then placed back into the cake. He marked the part of the cake containing the fatal raisin, making sure he gave that piece to his victim.

THE PRIM AND PROPER POISONER

If you lived in Victorian England you were either a have or a have-not. It was a period in history when the distinction between the two groups was never more distinct. To be of the genteel upper class one led a pampered life devoted to the conformity of the day.

The world stopped at tea time. You received your mail on a silver salver. Your maids brought you everything. To stoop or exert oneself was thought exceedingly rude. The vulgarity of actually handling money was avoided. One paid one's tradesman by having him leave his "book" every three months or so. The lady of the house would see that a cheque for the full amount was in the "book" which was picked up on the occasion of the next delivery.

This was not to say that Victorians didn't occasionally dispose of their wives, husbands or lovers. Heaven forbid, no era of history has been free from these rather routine crimes.

It may be said that, generally speaking, this class of English society did not lend itself to unique murderers. It is distressing to report in this day of women's liberation that the one unique and original murderer that did exist was a woman.

In 1871, Brighton, then as now, was an extremely popular seaside resort. The old homes, many of which are still standing, are now used as flats. Over 100 years ago many of them were occupied by one family.

Mrs. Edmunds and her little girl lived in one of them. Her little girl, Christiana, was a 43-year-old virgin, who was, as Noel Coward used to say "exceedingly on the shelf." You see, Christiana like the house, was neat, tidy and extremely boring. The only two men who ventured around were the vicar and the doctor. Now the very thought of anything as sexy as pounding surf would have given the old vicar a bad case of hives. Such was not the case with the doctor. Dr. Beard was in his early 40s, good looking, pleasant, sexy; but alas, he was married. Not only was he married, but it appears that he was happily married, which in some circles deserves distinction.

The doctor suspected that Christiana sought out his medical services when really she was looking for something quite different. Be that as it may, the doctor would have none of it and treated Christiana as he would any other patient. What the doctor didn't know was that Christiana was madly in love with him. She never spoke to her mother or anyone else of her love for the doctor. We only know of her turmoil in the light of later events.

From her desperate position, and in her distraught state, she reasoned that the doctor would really fall for her if he didn't have that cumbersome Mrs. Beard around her neck. Under the pretense of having to kill some bothersome cats, she purchased a supply of strychnine. The next time the good doctor and his wife came to tea she gave Mrs. Beard a chocolate laced with strychnine. Soon Mrs. Beard collapsed. The doctor seemed to realize what was happening. He immediately induced vomiting and saved his wife's life.

Dr. Beard was upset, as well may be expected, and refused to treat either mother or daughter again. He made the decision not to report the attempted poisoning to the authorities. The topic was never mentioned by any of the participants who had tea in the Edmunds parlor that day.

At this point Christiana had gambled and lost. Had she dismissed the whole thing criminologists would not be studying her case for over 100 years. She made the decision that was to give her method a horror of originality and wantonness that is unsurpassed by any female criminal.

She sent four youngsters at different times, to buy chocolates at the local sweet shop. She gathered up the chocolates and injected them with poison. She then had the youngsters return with the candy saying they tasted bitter. In each case the boys returned with candy the shopkeeper had given them in exchange. In this way she succeeded in getting quite a large supply of poisoned candies in the shopkeeper's stock. Not satisfied with this, Christiana injected the good chocolates she now had, and dropped them in shops around Brighton, figuring that someone would pick them up and eat them.

The entire population became susceptible to the poison so readily available. Only one little boy, Sidney Barker, ate the chocolates in sufficient quantity and was dead within the hour. Many became violently ill. Christiana sent chocolates to herself and was a volunteer witness at the inquest into Sidney Barker's death. She testified that she too had become very sick after eating the chocolates. The jury said the little boy had died through misadventure.

Again Christiana was off the hook. She wasn't suspected of making half the town sick or of the boy's death. In her love-crazed mind she figured now that everyone was being poisoned, including herself, the doctor would realize he had been mistaken when he thought she had attempted to poison his wife. It is warped reasoning, but at the time Christiana was in such a mental state that she would do anything to get back in the good graces of the doctor.

Next she wrote to Sidney Barker's father beseeching him to sue the confectioner who had sold the poisoned candy. She tried to disguise her handwriting, but the police had no trouble tracing the writer. The authorities then found out about the four boys buying candy at the same shop and returning it.

Christiana Edmunds was arrested. Feeling against her was strong in Brighton. Every resident or visitor had been a potential victim. The site of the trial was moved to the Old Bailey in London.

The most distinguished doctors available appeared for the defense, arguing that as a middle aged spinster Christiana was insane at the time she committed her insane acts. The jury didn't agree. They only deliberated an hour and brought in a verdict of guilty. She was sentenced to death by hanging.

Her sentence was later commuted to life in the Broadmoor Lunatic Asylum. Many people who have visited this institution believe that for a woman of Miss Edmunds background, the former sentence would have been more humane.

A strange and special consideration was given to Christiana while in Broadmoor. Every six months her mother would come and visit her. Christiana was allowed to discard her drab asylum dress and don the dress she wore at her trial. A maid was provided and tea was served in the governor's study. Mother and daughter would nibble on small cakes as they discussed the weather, old friends, and state of the Empire. No distasteful topic was ever uttered by the two women.

This ritual continued till the day Mrs. Edmunds received word that her daughter had died in the asylum.

THE MYSTERY LINGERS ON

Even today the name Marie Lafarge conjures up images of a dark chateau in France, a murdered husband, and a sensational trial. Over 100 years later criminolgists are still uncertain as to the answer to the perplexing problem: Did Marie really do it?

Born in France, Marie was a ward of her uncle and aunt. Uncle was an executive of the Banque de France, and, to put it mildly, was loaded. Marie was brought up with the finer things of life. She was, however, not blessed with a pleasing countenance. While not exactly ugly, Marie had a long, rather thin nose which was almost constantly dripping. From the neck down Marie was just great. A large dowry awaited any man willing to overlook the perpetual drip.

In 1839 Marie's uncle and aunt had a heart to heart chat concerning the lack of men in their ward's life. Being of a practical nature Auntie decided to advertise, seeking a husband for her 23-year-old niece.

Charles Pouch Lafarge applied for the position and was accepted. It is only fair to point out that Charles was exactly twice Marie's age. A coarse, gruff man, who was an ironmonger by trade, he was many other things by inclination. Charles thought that overindulgence in eating, drinking, and sex was the only thing in life.

Gentle, protected Marie and rough tough Charles were married in August, 1839. The ceremony was barely concluded before Charles bundled up his new bride and carted her off to his chateau in Glandier. Marie was greeted at the chateau by Charles' mother and sister. The realization that they would be living with her was bad enough, but the appearance of the chateau was even worse. It was an old rat infested mansion in an advanced state of decay.

That very first night Charles ingratiated himself with his new wife by eating like a pig, drinking like a camel, and snoring like a lion. Marie realized that she had made a terrible mistake. The more she thought of it the more she knew she would never let this coarse man have her body. The future looked bleak. Marie wanted out.

She decided to write Charles a letter. It is too long a missive to reproduce here, but the following excerpts will give you the general idea:

> "Charles, on my knees I ask your forgiveness. I have deceived you terribly. I do not love you. I love another. He is handsome; he is noble. We were brought up together. We have loved each other since we were able to love anything.
>
> Poor me! I thought a kiss on the forehead would be all you would expect. Habit and training have put an immense barrier between us. In place of gentle words of love and sweet nothings, there are these feelings which take voice in you and which revolt me."

When Charles opened the letter you could hear the screaming and cursing on the other side of the channel. His mother and sister had to restrain him. Of course, there was no other man in Marie's life, but in her own way she managed to achieve the concession she sought. From then on Marie and Charles spent their nights in separate bedrooms.

Charles, having demonstrated his anger at this celibate turn of events, gradually decided that in order to keep Marie and her considerable dowry he had better calm down. Marie, too, decided to make the best of an awkward situation. Like many couples before them they drifted into a life of quiet desperation. Charles shared his thoughts with Marie, who dutifully displayed a more than passing interest in her husband, his hobbies and his business. To the outside world they appeared to be a happy, devoted couple.

At about this time in their marriage, Charles' iron business began to sour. Having lived so long with a degree of security, it now preyed on his mind that he might lose everything. To make matters worse, Marie took ill. Nothing serious, but cause for some concern. Charles was really touched when he was informed that while ill, Marie had made out a will leaving everything she possessed to him. So touched was he that he made out his own will, leaving everything to his wife. Marie quickly recovered.

Unfortunately, unlike Marie's illness, Charles' business problems didn't go away. There was one ray of sunshine in an otherwise dark future. Charles purchased the rights to a patent concerning the manufacture of iron, which he felt was worth a fortune, if only he could interest financiers in the venture.

At this juncture in their marriage Marie and Charles were truly concerned with each other's welfare. Certainly Charles figured that once his patent was accepted and proven, he would be wealthy beyond his wildest dreams. He and Marie spent their evenings talking about luxurious trips, homes in Italy, and clothing fit for royalty.

Off Charles went to Paris for a prolonged business trip to see if he could interest the money boys in his patent. Since it was just before Christmas Marie baked a lovely cake for her husband. She placed it into a Christmas parcel, in which she also affectionately placed a new pair of socks, a pair of slippers, and most touching of all, a picture of herself.

Upon receipt of the parcel Charles knocked off most of the cake in one sitting. Within hours he was suffering from terrible stomach pains. In a few days the pains subsided.

After the turn of the year Charles became convinced that his mission to raise money had met with failure. He returned to Glandier.

A few days after his homecoming his stomach pains returned. A doctor was immediately summoned. He prescribed several different medicines, none of which seemed to do any good. Marie personally insisted on tending to her husband's every wish during his illness. She spoonfed the weakened man, but despite this gentle care every meal was followed by violent bouts of vomiting.

Charles' mother had comforted her daughter-in-law throughout the family crisis. Now she intuitively felt that something was rotten. What's more, she thought that something was Marie. It appeared to her that Marie was just too insistent on taking care of Charles. Once she thought she saw Marie drop some white powder into her son's broth. Marie purchased a packet of arsenic, ostensibly to reduce the rat population of the chateau.

Enough is enough. Charles' mother told her son of her suspicions. Charles, despite his weakened condition, was at first furious with his mother. When Mummie actually showed him the whitish sediment at the bottom of a cup at his bedside, he realized that her suspicions were well founded.

A doctor was called, and he quickly tested for the presence of arsenic. The sediment in the cup proved to be arsenic, but the discovery was too late to save Charles. He had been systematically poisoned for far too long. Next day he was dead.

Charles' mother contacted the police the moment her boy closed his eyes. The post mortem revealed that Charles' death was due to arsenic poisoning. Marie was arrested and later stood trial for the murder of her husband. In all the history of crime it remains as one of the most publicized murder trials ever held.

The case against Marie appeared to be airtight. Her gift of the Christmas cake, followed by her husband's illness, weighed heavily against her. Her purchase of arsenic, which she never fed to the chateau rats, was also difficult to explain. It was also proven at her trial that she alone prepared all of Charles' food during his illness. Marie was found guilty and received a sentence of life imprisonment.

From the moment of her confinement at Montpelier, Marie's lawyers began their struggle to free her. They were assisted by the work of a well-known chemist, who took an interest in the case. Monsieur Raspail purchased the same experimental equipment which the authorities had used to prove that Charles had died of arsenic poisoning. He was amazed to discover that some of the zinc gauze used in the experiment contained arsenic.

It is not easy to interfere with a French jury's decision. Year after year Marie's lawyers worked diligently to establish her innocence. In 1852, after 12 long years in confinement, Marie was given a full pardon.

Old friends took her to a resort to recover from the hardships of prison, but to no avail. Her will to live was gone. Marie Lafarge died a few months after her release.

MYSTERIOUS MURDER OF WEALTHY LANDOWNER

In order to fully comprehend the singularly unsatisfactory Bravo case, it is necessary for us to dwell for a moment on the personalities involved and their relationship to one another.

Come back with me to Victorian England and meet my cast of characters. Florence Campbell was a good looking young girl of 19 when she met and married a Captain Ricardo. Florence and the handsome captain tied the knot in 1864, and almost immediately the anticipated connubial bliss started to fade. The captain preferred the bottle over Florence's considerable charms. Rather than go through a divorce, the couple decided on a separation. In conjunction with their separate living accommodations, Florence was to receive an allowance of 1,200 pounds per year. In 1871 the valiant captain died of natural causes. Being preoccupied with the consumption of alcoholic beverages as he was, Ricardo neglected to change his will before his demise. The will had been drawn up immediately following his wedding day. Florence hit the jackpot—she was left with an income of 4,000 pounds per year.

Florence moved into a large house, The Priory, on Bedford Hill Road in Balham. Into this house she brought her paid companion, a Jamaican lady, Mrs. Jane Cannon Cox, who was an interesting soul, to say the least. Florence had met Mrs. Cox by a roundabout route. Sometime before, Mrs. Cox's husband had died in Jamaica, leaving her almost penniless. A Mr. Joseph Bravo, a wealthy landowner and businessman on the island, took an interest in the widow Cox. He was instrumental in sending her three children to school in England. She later followed the children, and hired out as a daily governess to provide herself with an income. She became acquainted with the children of friends of Mrs. Ricardo, and in this way entered Florence's life. The two widows took a liking to each other. It was quite natural for Florence to hire Mrs. Cox as a companion at a salary of 100 pounds a year.

When Florence moved into the Priory with Mrs. Cox one must realize that in a few short years Mrs. Cox's station in life had taken a turn for the better. From being stuck in Jamaica without husband or funds and with three small children, she now was a dear friend and companion of a wealthy woman in a huge house. She held court over a large staff of servants. The rolling grounds came complete with horses and carriages. Mrs. Cox never had it so good.

Whenever her benefactor, Mr. Bravo was in England, Mrs. Cox would visit with the Bravo family. One day she brought Florence with her. On this particular summer day Florence met Mr. and Mrs. Bravo and their son Charles. Whatever attracts people to one another was at work that day. Charles took to Florence like a duck takes to water. Florence took to Charles in much the same manner. We can only wonder if the fact that Charles had an endowment of 20,000 pounds payable to him upon the death of his last surviving parent, had anything to do with the torrid romance which followed. About the only thing that marred the whole affair was Mrs. Bravo's distinct dislike of Florence. Such a minor obstacle was overlooked and within a few months Charles and Florence were married.

In January, 1876 we find Charles and Florence, accompanied by the ever faithful Mrs. Cox, comfortably ensconced in The Priory. On Tuesday, April 18 of that year, events were to take place in this house that were to place all our characters under minute examination. The English-speaking world was to follow their every utterance with meticulous care.

At 4 o'clock that afternoon Charles decided to take one of his horses for a ride. At half past seven Mrs. Cox returned from shopping, and joined Charles and Florence for dinner. The evening meal had as its main course lamb with poached eggs on toast. All three participants ate a hearty meal. A butler decanted the wine, which we are told consisted of one bottle of Marsala, one bottle of Burgundy and two bottles of sherry. Not bad for three people. Those Victorians knew how to live.

At about a quarter to nine the ladies, somewhat drowsy after a good meal and the wine, retired for the night. They were soon followed by Charles who went to his own bedroom which joined that of his wife. The housemaid, Mary Ann Keeber, entered her mistress' dressing room, put away Florence's clothing and tidied up. Then she started to go down the stairs. She was standing in the hallway, when, all of a sudden Charles' door flew open. He rushed into the hall shouting, "Florence! Florence! Hot water! Hot water!" Mary Ann, scared out of her wits, summoned Mrs. Cox. In the meantime Charles had returned to his room and was violently vomiting out a window. Mrs. Cox sent Mary Ann for water and mustard. By the time she returned to the room Charles had passed out on the floor and Mrs. Cox was massaging his chest. Busy Mrs. Cox then dispatched a coachman to fetch a Dr. Harrison.

Mary Ann woke up Florence, who said with an utter disregard for originality, "What is the matter?" After she came to her senses she fetched a Dr. Moore, who lived closer than Dr. Harrison. Dr. Moore was the first man of medicine to arrive on the scene. He examined Charles and could barely detect a pulse. Dr. Moore, who can be admired for his bluntness, if not his bedside manner, stated, that in his opinion, the patient was suffering from the administration of poison and the family could expect the worst.

Dr. Harrison then showed up. He was met by Mrs. Cox, who greeted him with the words, "I am sure he has taken chloroform." Because of this startling declaration, the two doctors searched the room and came up with three bottles; one containing chloroform, one laudanum, and one camphor liniment. The doctors then brought in two more colleagues who agreed that the patient had been poisoned.

At three in the morning Charles regained consciousness, and despite being in extreme pain, he was able to answer the doctors' questions. He admitted rubbing his gums with laudanum as a treatment for neuralgia. The doctors told him this couldn't possibly account for his condition. Charles said, "I have taken nothing else. If it was not laudanum, I don't know what it was."

At this point Mrs. Cox had a private consultation with one of the four doctors—Dr. Johnson. She said that Charles had told her, "I've taken some of that poison, but don't tell Florence." When approached with this information Charles repeated that he had only taken laudanum for his gums, and nothing else.

On Wednesday the dying man asked his family, which was now reinforced with the presence of his mother and father, to join him in the Lord's Prayer. Two days later, after 56 hours of suffering, Charles Bravo died. His last words were, "Be kind to my darling wife, mother; she has been the best of wives to me."

An inquiry into the death was held on April 25 at the Priory. Refreshments were served, and the matter was disposed of quietly and quickly. One disconcerting note was the wording of the jury's verdict: "That the deceased died from the effects of poison, but we have not sufficient evidence under what circumstances it came into his body."

When the facts surrounding the mysterious death became public, there was a great hue and cry for further investigation. The case became such a matter of conjecture that it ended up being argued in the House of Commons. Finally, the coroner was ordered to hold a new inquiry. On July 11 the second inquest was held at the Bedford Hotel in Balham. When called to testify, Mrs. Cox now stated that Charles had said to her, "Mrs. Cox, I have taken poison for Gully, don't tell Florence."

You might well ask—who in the world is Gully? In 1870, while Florence was still Mrs. Ricardo, she became attracted to Dr. James Manby Gully, a man old enough to be her father. Attraction led to deception, and deception led to you know what. The affair continued through the time of poor Captain Ricardo's death right up to her engagement to Charles Bravo. Before she married Charles, Florence told him of the intimate relationship which had existed between herself and the elderly doctor. She and the doctor returned gifts they had given to each other, and both agreed to end the affair. Florence stated that her husband promised never to let her past come between them, but almost immediately he started accusing her of still carrying on with Dr. Gully, which she swore was not the case. Mrs. Cox and Florence had thus provided a motive for suicide, and at the same time, one might argue, a motive for murder. Despite the two ladies' statements, everyone else connected with Charles Bravo depicted him as a jovial, hearty man who loved life and was a poor candidate for suicide.

Dr. Gully was dragged through the inquest and suspicion was cast in his direction, for he had a motive. He may very well have changed his mind and wanted to continue his dalliance with Florence. While he wasn't in the house on the fateful night, he could have coerced Florence or Mrs. Cox to administer the poison.

Did Mrs. Cox receive pressure from Charles to leave the house, as some claimed? Did she see the good life slipping away and decide to do something about it? Mrs. Cox did call Dr. Harrison to the scene, knowing full well that Dr. Moore lived closer to The Priory.

Even though almost everyone agrees that Charles did not commit suicide, it is always possible, taking into consideration that people act in strange ways. This theory begs a question. Why did he not admit it when he was told that he was going to die anyway? Then, again, Charles' letters to his relatives were read at the inquest. In them he praised his loving wife.

*   *   *

The inquest jury stated:

"We find that Mr. Charles Bravo did not commit suicide; that he did not meet his death by misadventure; that he was willfully murdered by the administration of poison; but there is not sufficient evidence to fix the guilt on any person or persons."

No one ever stood trial for the murder of Charles Bravo. Dr. Gully passed away shortly after the inquest. Florence Bravo disappeared from public view. There are those who say she died heartbroken within a year. Mrs. Cox returned to Jamaica and was never heard of again.

PART 2

THE CANADIANS

WHO KILLED MRS. HENNING?

Murder from a distance can be objective and academic. Vicious acts can be studied and appraised and, as an antique dealer looks at a rare vase judging its authenticity, the student of murder can turn over in his mind the many aspects of a sensational murder case. What was the real motive? Was it money? Was it sex? What made it sensational?

In actual fact, when a murder occurs, it is the most personal of all acts. Certainly to the killer, the victim, and the many people whose lives they touch, nothing could be more personal and tragic.

The police who hunt these killers get up in the morning and go to work. While many of us build houses, and sell toothpaste, and provide all the necessary services that make this world go around, the police go to work to find someone who has taken that most precious of all possessions—life itself. Many other law enforcement officers protect, but not these men. They apprehend.

The Ontario Provincial Police have jurisdiction over 17 districts in Ontario. Whenever a major crime is committed, assistance is readily available from the Criminal Investigation Branch headquarters in Toronto. From headquarters, Ontario's top detectives are assigned to coordinate investigations into major crimes, wherever they may occur in the province.

The ringing of the telephone woke Detective Inspector Ron Kendrick from a deep sleep. He glanced at his watch, it was 4 a.m. While he didn't expect a call when he went to bed the previous night, he knew he could receive one at any time. Like a doctor, Inspector Kendrick was "on call". It was the early morning hours of Sept. 20, 1975. Someone in a village called Ayton had found a body in a service station.

He had phoned in his grim discovery to No. 6 District Headquarters in Mt. Forest. The detective sergeant in Mt. Forest drove 10 miles to the scene, and after verifying that indeed a murder had taken place, he notified his superintendent. Now the superintendent was on the other end of the line to Kendrick.

Ron Kendrick is a strapping, 6 ft. 1 inch career policeman. He has had only one job in his life, and he is still at it. He joined the police force when he was 19-years-old, and now is a veteran with more than 20 years service on the force.

Inspector Kendrick drove west along Highway 401 to Highway 6, where he made a right turn and headed north. His headlights picked out small sleeping towns as he sped past. Fergus, Arthur, Kenilworth, and finally Mt. Forest. Just a few miles past Mt. Forest, Grey County Sideroad No. 9 turns off Highway 6 to the left toward Ayton. It is 10 miles from Highway 6 along this road to Ayton. Daylight illuminated the rural landscape as Kendrick drove through the tiny town. The 400 souls who live there were hardly stirring as he pulled up among the several police cars already parked in front of Henning's BP Gas station and lunch counter. He looked at his watch, it was 7:30 a.m.

Lincoln Becker is 38-years-old. He receives a pension because of an industrial accident he once suffered. In Ayton you can usually find Lincoln helping out at the other BP station which is situated in the centre of town. From force of habit Lincoln usually ended his day with a cup of coffee out R.R. #1 at Mrs. Henning's lunch counter. On the night of Sept. 19 he joked and passed the time with Mrs. Henning. She was cheerful and good natured like always. Shortly after 11 o'clock Lincoln left the lunch counter, said good night and walked out the door. Mrs. Henning locked up behind him.

Lincoln Becker was the last known person to see Aleitha Jane Henning alive.

Inspector Kendrick examined the body lying on the floor in the service station portion of the Henning establishment.

Mrs. Henning, a 58-year-old widow, had been severely beaten about the head. A great deal of blood emanated from head wounds. Later Dr. Ray Sawchuk, a pathologist, confirmed that a skull fracture was the cause of death. She had been stabbed several times in the chest. Mrs. Henning was fully dressed, wearing a blouse and slacks. She had not been sexually molested in any way. Her blouse was pulled up to just below the rib cage, exposing the area above the abdomen to the bottom of the rib cage. Here the killer started a slash from her side across the front of her body. At approximately the halfway point in this gaping wound the killer either extracted the knife and then continued on, or for some reason changed the direction of the knife cut slightly. Mrs. Henning was already dead from a fractured skull when she was stabbed and slashed.

On the lunch counter was the coffee cup used by Lincoln Becker the night before. Mrs. Henning had been killed before she had a chance to wash it.

For two months Ron Kendrick lived with the senseless Henning murder. He knew every minute detail of the victim's life. The Hennings had been in Ayton for approximately 20 years. Mr. Henning passed away six years previously and his wife carried on the family business. They had two children, a daughter, 22, married and living in Kitchener and a son, 27, married and living a few miles from Ayton. He had two children whom his mother adored. Mrs. Henning's family could shed no light on who would want to do this horrible thing to their mother. The victim was a church going, hard working individual. She didn't drink or take drugs. There were no men in her life. She was good natured and obliging.

The absence of a motive made the case difficult to solve. Nothing was touched in the garage or lunch counter. There was money in the cash register that was not disturbed.

Ron Kendrick says, "It's like someone walked in, killed her, and walked out."

The premises were locked and the one thing that everyone agrees on is that Mrs. Henning was security conscious. Once she locked up she wouldn't let anyone in unless she knew him. The assumption is that someone in the area is the killer.

With the help of six policemen working full time on the case, Inspector Kendrick managed to question an entire town. A reward was posted offering $5,000 for information leading to the arrest and conviction of the killer. The medical profile points to a schizophrenic.

Ron Kendrick feels that the out of the way location of

Ayton, coupled with the fact that the killer was probably known to the victim, made the entire case a complicated and different one.

As I drove through the small Ontario towns, I thought back to the early morning hours of the day when Inspector Kendrick had made the same trip. I swung off Highway 6 and drove west along No. 9. I realized why the police were so sure the killer is from the district. There simply is no reason to go to Ayton late at night. To travel north or south you don't go through the town. Travelling east or west you would simply take a more convenient and better road.

The signs have been taken down from Mrs. Henning's service station. For security reasons a lone perpetual light replaced the lighted gas pumps and lunch counter. Directly across from the service station the new Normanby Central School stands out as the most modern building in town.

Who would kill and mutilate a woman who had never done any harm to anyone in her life?

The people of the small community are friendly enough, but they are guarded in the statements they make. Nothing of this magnitude had ever happened in the town before. There are very few people who live a few months or years in Ayton and move on, like in the big city. Most are citizens of long standing and everyone knows everyone else extremely well. They have been unnerved by questions from police and reporters. Above all, the thought of a vicious killer still among them is hard to accept.

I spoke to many of the townspeople and they were willing to talk to me only if I agreed not to have their pictures taken and not to use their names.

One lady remembered the last time tragedy had struck their town. Her father told her the story about two cattle drovers who had an argument. One hit the other over the head with a cane and killed him. That was in 1919. She told me that in that case, of course, the killer was known. No real violence had broken the peacefulness of the community for more than 56 years.

She continued, "You know, no one around here ever bothered to lock up their homes at night. There didn't seem to be any reason, but things have changed. We all do now."

A businessman in town told me, "In a small place like this we all knew Mrs. Henning very well. Everyone can remember the last time they saw her. It's strange how everyone remembers how pleasant and cheerful she was now that she is gone."

Another man said, "Everytime I talk to a stranger I get the feeling they think I killed Mrs. Henning. That's why everyone in town doesn't like being questioned."

A garage operator wasn't so amicable. "Why don't you guys drop it? Let it be. No one can undo this thing now. Let the police catch the guy and the town can go back to the way it was before."

Shock, anger, sorrow, and dismay register clearly with these people. This is not the impersonal non-involvement of a large city. A way of life was disrupted that is the backbone of rural Ontario.

The citizens of Ayton can't really comprehend why, late on the night of Sept. 19, or in the early morning hours of Sept. 20, a madman descended on a tiny service station in their tiny town, and for no apparent reason viciously took the life of one of their own.

I can't either.

AUTHOR'S NOTE:
Three years after Mrs. Henning's murder an individual was apprehended and tried for the Henning murder. He was acquitted and the case remains unsolved.

THE TORSO ON THE MOUNTAIN

"We've found a dead man! Part of a dead man!" shouted Bob Weaver, age 10 and his brother Fred, 9, to their friends.

From the moment these words were spoken on March 16, 1946 no other crime ever perpetrated in Canada captured the imagination of the Canadian public as did what was to become known as the Evelyn Dick Case. From Antigonish, Nova Scotia to Port Alberni, British Columbia everyone followed the exploits of a handful of characters who told unbelievable and horrible stories of what took place in the days and months before the youngsters' gruesome discovery on Hamilton Mountain.

The body was without arms, legs and head. Two days after it was found Alexander Kammerer reported that a roomer of his, John Dick, was missing since March 6. Dick, who worked for the Hamilton Street Railway Co. as a conductor, had not shown up for work that day. The police located his wife, Evelyn, who lived at 32 Carrick Ave. She could throw no light on the disappearance, except to volunteer that she and her husband were living apart. They were married only five months. The next day, two brothers of John Dick positively identified the body as that of their missing brother. Mrs. Dick was now questioned more closely. She gave the first of her many statements.

Evelyn said she married John Dick using the name Evelyn White. She told him her husband was a navy man who had passed away, and that she had a retarded daughter Heather, age 4, who had been fathered by White. Evelyn admitted to having affairs with other men while married to Dick, but claimed that he saw other women as well. Then she told the most fantastic tale of all. She related how she had received a phone call instructing her to borrow a car. The caller told

60

her he was a member of a hired gang who had been retained to kill her husband. The mysterious caller said the reason her husband must die was because he had been seeing another man's wife, and made an appointment to meet her on Claremont Dr. on March 6. She borrowed a Packard and when she arrived at the appointed spot the man was there with a heavy sack. After placing the sack in the back seat, he got in the Packard and the two drove away. The stranger volunteered that the sack contained a part of John Dick.

Finally they arrived at the mountain and the stranger dumped the contents of the sack on the ground. Evelyn said she became sick. The man tossed the body over the edge of a bank. She let her mysterious passenger off at the Royal Connaught Hotel and returned the Packard to its owner. To account for the blood in the vehicle, Evelyn wrote a note to the owner of the car saying that her little girl cut her finger. The police proceeded to check 331 Carrick Ave. Here they found pictures of handsome Bill Bohozuc. They also found bank books containing large balances and a bloodstained skirt of Evelyn's.

Evelyn was detained by the police. In the meantime the authorities started to uncover the tumultuous life led by the main characters in our cast. First and foremost there was beautiful Evelyn, with long black hair and a natural flirtatious look that oozed charisma. She lived on Carrick Ave. with her mother, Mrs. Donald MacLean and her 4-year-old daughter, Heather. Her father lived at 214 Rosslyn Ave. He too, was living apart from his wife. When his home was searched police found a revolver and ammunition, as well as an axe, saws, and a butcher knife. The house also contained enough incriminating evidence to charge him with theft from his employer, the Hamilton Street Railway Co.

Bill Bohozuc, the handsome other man in Evelyn's life, was found to own a revolver as well.

The more the police poked around, the more suspect everyone became. The police even found a bloody necktie in the back seat of the Packard Evelyn had borrowed. Mrs. Dick now changed her story and claimed that she witnessed the shooting of her husband by one Anthony Romanelli. This story was still news when she gave out a statement that it too was false. A more thorough search of the now infamous house at 32 Carrick Ave. uncovered a bushel basket of ashes. Later these ashes were found to contain bits of bone and teeth. The missing parts of John Dick had been cremated in the furnace. It seems that every time a search was instituted at the house new evidence was uncovered.

On Friday, March 22, the whole affair blew wide open. The police found a ladies' beige travelling case in the house. When the lock was broken it was discovered that the case contained a cardboard carton filled with cement. Under the supervision of a pathologist, Dr. W. J. Deadman, the cement was chipped away to reveal the body of a newborn baby boy. There was a cord fastened around the infant's neck.

Evelyn was quick to give her third statement. This time she told of bad feeling between her husband and Bill Bohozuc. She was having sexual relations with Bohozuc, and her husband strongly suspected them. John Dick had kept telling everyone about the affair, but other than drive Bohozuc half crazy, he didn't do anything about it. She stated that Bohozuc told her he had killed her husband. She claimed he even brought some of the pieces of the body over to her home and put them in the little garage beside the house, to be later burned in the furnace.

While Evelyn continued to make statements, the investigation was grinding out more grisly facts. The baby in the cement was the child of Evelyn and Bill Bohozuc. She had given birth to a boy in September of 1944 at the Mount Hamilton Hospital. The very day she was discharged from the hospital, she claimed Bill Bohozuc placed a cord around the baby's neck and strangled it. She made further statements incriminating her father, saying he and her husband argued bitterly.

In the end Evelyn Dick stood trial for the murder of her husband. She was found Guilty on Oct. 16, 1946, and was sentenced to hang. Her counsel immediately advised the court that there would be an appeal for a new trial. The following day, Oct. 17, Bill Bohozuk and Evelyn's father, Donald MacLean, stood trial for the same murder. One of the main witnesses to be called at their trial was none other than Evelyn. When this occurred, she refused to give evidence. It was felt she refused because she was appealing her case, and did not want to prejudice her chances. The judge was compelled to discharge the jury and delay the proceedings.

Evelyn's lawyer, J. J. Robinette, won the appeal for a new

trial. It started on Feb. 24, 1947, and Robinette leaned heavily toward her father being the actual murderer. This time the jury brought in a verdict of Not Guilty. While everyone realized she had guilty knowledge of the crime, it was felt that there was a reasonable doubt as to whether she actually killed her husband.

Only four days later, she was back in court facing a new charge, that of murdering her own child. This time the prosecution proved that Evelyn left her home with a live baby and returned with a locked travelling case. The jury brought in a verdict of Not Guilty of murder, but Guilty of manslaughter. She was sentenced to life imprisonment.

The next trial was that of Bill Bohozuk for the murder of the baby. He claimed he was not the father of the child, and had never killed the baby. Another field day for the press occurred when Mrs. Bill Bohozuk showed up. No one was aware that he was married. She had been living in the United States for months. Mrs. Bohozuk stated that she was with her husband all day on the date Evelyn claimed he had strangled the child. The jury obviously believed her. They took only ten minutes to find him Not Guilty.

Both Donald MacLean and Bill Bohozuk then stood trial for the murder of John Dick. When Mrs. Dick again refused to testify the judge instructed the jury to bring in a verdict of Not Guilty pertaining to Bohozuk. This they did without leaving the jury box. Donald MacLean heard all the same evidence one more time. He was finally acquitted of murder, but was convicted of being an accessory after the fact of murder. MacLean received a sentence of five years in prison.

No one was ever convicted of murdering John Dick and cutting off his arms, legs and head.

Epilogue

Whatever happened to all the characters in this tangled, fascinating case?

Mrs. Donald MacLean took little Heather and moved away from Hamilton.

Donald MacLean spent four years in Kingston Penitentiary and was released in 1951. He worked for some time as a parking lot attendant, and died in 1955.

Bill Bohozuk's whereabouts are unknown.

Evelyn Dick served 11 years in prison, and was paroled in 1958. She has disappeared from view.

MURDER IN THE BATHTUB

As teenagers Jane Whelpley and Terrence Milligan both
attended school in Saint John, N. B. The youngsters never
met in the Maritimes and had no way of knowing they
would travel over a thousand miles to meet, marry, and
encounter tragedy in Toronto.

Det. Donald Wright arrived at Terrence and Jane Milligan's apartment only half an hour after the police received a
phone call from Terrence telling them that his wife was
dead. It was 8 a.m. Sunday, June 11, 1967. Upon entering
the apartment located at Eglinton Ave. E. and Birchmount in
Toronto's east end, Wright found Jane Milligan dead in her
bath. He immediately had an instinctive feeling that all was
not as it should be. The bathtub had a barren look that was
not typical. Wright's trained detective's eye noticed that there
was no soap or facecloth near the tub. Jane Milligan's body
was sitting in the tub with her back to the taps. While there
is no rule that dictates how a person sits in a bathtub, Wright
correctly deduced that the vast majority of people sit in a
bathtub facing the taps. A mantle radio was lying in the tub
in a foot of water beside the body.

The obvious conclusion was that death was due to electrocution. Wright scanned the scene and noticed that an extension cord had been used to plug the radio into an outlet in
the livingroom. This allowed Jane to place the radio on the
edge of the tub. Without using the extension cord she could
have plugged the radio into an outlet in the bathroom, ena-
bling her to place it in a safer location.

Would it be natural for Jane to go through the inconvenience of using an extension cord in order to place the radio
on such an obviously dangerous perch?

Milligan told Wright that his blonde, 19-year-old wife had

awakened him at about 6 a.m. She asked him if he wanted breakfast. He declined and went back to sleep. When he awoke at 7:30 a.m., he called out to her but received no answer. He got up to look for his wife. He told Det. Wright that he found his wife dead in the bathtub. He said he pulled out the plug of the radio before touching her body. Within 10 minutes, under the inquisitive but still gentle questioning of the detective, Milligan changed his story. He now said he didn't even notice the radio but touched his wife's body to see if there were any signs of life. When Wright suggested that he must have received a shock, Milligan volunteered that he was mistaken—no doubt he had unplugged the radio first.

Over and above Milligan's elaborate stories, Wright was amazed that the 22-year-old could be so composed after finding his wife dead only minutes before. The couple had been married less than a year. Milligan, who seemed to be a lucid, clean-cut young man, casually mentioned to Wright that he had a $15,000 double indemnity policy on his wife's life. He stood to collect $30,000 from the unfortunate accident.

After two and a half hours in Milligan's company, Wright came to the private conclusion that he had walked into a murder case. Within days Det. Wright had his vacation postponed. He was assigned to the Milligan investigation.

Wright checked the neighborhood to get a profile on Terry Milligan. The Milligan's immediate neighbor, Mrs. Marion Bakes, said she had often heard fighting from the young couple's apartment. She said that early in the morning of Jane's death, she had heard a rubbing noise, like the sound of flesh against porcelain, but had heard no loud noise or music from the adjacent apartment. Wright recalled that when the radio was recovered from the water the volume indicator was at the high position.

While Wright was becoming more convinced than ever that he had stumbled across murder, the pathologist's office released the cause of death—asphyxiation, probably due to electrocution. Wright couldn't believe it. He was sure the scene had been set up to give the impression of death by accidental electrocution. The detective was convinced that the cause of death was drowning.

Jane Milligan was buried, and that very same day Det.

Wright received a call from the Toronto General Hospital. Terry was in the emergency ward suffering from exhaustion and alcohol. He had collapsed on a busy downtown Toronto street. Wright rushed to the hospital, thinking in the back of his mind that his suspect may have broken and was ready to confess. He did not find a repentant Milligan. Instead the baby-faced suspect accused the police of trying to invent evidence to convict him of murder. Later it was discovered that Milligan had an IQ of 135, which placed him in the near genius class. This day the bereaved husband not very cleverly took Wright into his confidence and inquired where he could find a prostitute.

Wright checked into Jane Milligan's background, and found nothing unusual. She had finished Grade 12 and had been employed as a teller in a Scarborough bank.

While all the incriminating circumstantial evidence uncovered by Wright indicated foul play, the pathologist's report could not be denied. It stated emphatically that death was due to asphyxiation, probably caused by electrocution. There is something about an official report that seems to defy questioning. Despite this, Det. Wright decided to delve further into the pathologist's report. This may have been the single most important decision of the entire investigation. Wright found out that the pathologist had made only a cursory examination of the remains. He had been in a hurry to go to a medical convention in Montreal. A few scribbled notes were, in the main, what went to make up the report. Fortunately, Jane's vital organs had been retained after her body had been buried.

A second examination of the organs was conducted, and a quite different cause of death was discovered—death due to drowning, no evidence of electrocution. In addition, the new report included other information not previously mentioned. There were bruises to the body below the left eye, on the left elbow, and hip.

An inquest was called for July 27, 1967, and the police feverishly tracked down witnesses. Wright questioned employees at two electrical plants where Milligan worked. Both Sangamo Co. Ltd. in Leaside and Crouse-Hinds Co. of Canada Ltd. in Scarborough had large staffs. Wright located some workers who knew Milligan well and were willing to testify that he referred to his wife as "the old bitch". In fact, some specifically stated that Terry used to go out of his way to let them know that his wife was terribly careless about placing her radio on the edge of the bathtub.

On June 21 Milligan was served with a subpoena to appear at the inquest into his wife's death on July 27. When given the subpoena he informed the authorities that he was leaving Toronto to live with his uncle on a farm in Prince Edward Island.

On July 27 Milligan returned to Toronto for the inquest. The jury determined that Mrs. Milligan's death was due to "homicide at the hands of her husband". Terrence Milligan was arrested and charged with non capital murder. Det. Wright's job was now over. He turned his thick file on the Milligan case over to Det. Sgt. Jim Crawford and Det. Sgt. Jack Evans, whose job it was to prove murder in a court of law.

The two detectives went over all the ground that Wright had already covered. They received the co-operation of Sangamo and Crouse-Hinds officials, and had offices made available to them in each plant. They stayed almost a week at each location, questioning employees. They found out that Milligan had implanted the idea of a radio in the bathtub to several of his co-workers. He insinuated that his wife was careless with the radio. Yet none of his neighbors in the east end of the city had ever heard him even mention this fact. Was he cunning enough to avoid bringing up this subject to his neighbors, perhaps fearful that they would mention it to his wife?

Crawford flew to Prince Edward Island with a search warrant to go through Milligan's belongings on his uncle's farm. One of his discoveries was a paperback book entitled "The Doomsters", by Ross MacDonald. Crawford's secretary later was to read the book and find out that two victims in the story met their deaths by having a radio thrown in the bathtub. Crawford, mindful that Milligan had spent the month before his arrest in Prince Edward Island, plodded across the countryside looking for friends of the accused. The islanders quickly identified the six foot four inch Crawford as the big cop from the city. Soon he located friends of Milligan's who told him that Terry was not your typical bereaved husband. He had taken out girls and attended dances only days after his wife's funeral.

Evans and Crawford tried balancing Milligan's radio on

the edge of the bathtub and found it very difficult. I know. I tried the same thing with the same radio on the same bathtub. Anyone with average intelligence would know that the slightest touch would either knock the radio to the floor or into the tub. Using any degree of common sense, you just wouldn't put a radio in such a precarious position.

Crawford and Evans had a plumber take the entire bathtub out of the apartment. The job was completed in eight hours, so as not to inconvenience the new tenants. They transported the tub to the basement at police headquarters. Policewoman Janet Ebert, clad only in a bathing suit, entered the bathtub. The water level was the same as the day Det. Wright walked into the Milligan apartment. Policewoman Ebert sat in the tub with her back to the taps, in the same position as Jane Milligan. She bent over and placed her head under the water. Later she verified that her head kept coming to the surface. She even tried to concentrate on keeping her head under water, but try as she might, there was a natural pressure for her head to bob to the surface.

Milligan's trial for non capital murder began on Monday, May 13, 1968. The prosecution succeeded in establishing that Jane met her death by drowning, not electrocution. The Crown paraded witness after witness to the stand, each one adding to the intertwined series of incidents that completely incriminated the accused.

David Keeler, who lived close by the Milligan apartment, testified how Terry had knocked on his door that fateful morning with the words, "My wife's drowning, let me call the police."

William Green, an electrical engineer, testified that anyone receiving an electrical shock while sitting in the bathtub, would certainly scream. Mrs. Bakes, the Milligan's immediate neighbor, who could hear the squeak of flesh on porcelain through the walls, testified that she heard no scream.

Eric Armstrong, a fellow employee of Milligan's at Sangamo, told of a strange conversation he had with Terry when he drove him home three weeks before his wife died. Armstrong said of the conversation, "He mentioned the fact that his wife was worth a lot of money, and he wouldn't mind doing away with her."

Even the manager of the cemetery where Milligan had picked out a plot for wife, took the stand. He quoted Milligan as saying, "It is probably better than she deserves."

Crawford and Evans had done their job well. The jury took 10½ hours to find Milligan guilty of non capital murder. The judge congratulated them on their verdict, and Terrence Milligan received life imprisonment, where he is confined to this day.

Staff Sgt. Jim Crawford, now 28 years a cop, vividly remembers the case that took place over 10 years ago. The huge man whose dogged police work was most responsible for placing Terrence Milligan behind bars, says with a note of distinct satisfaction in his voice, "It was certainly one of my most interesting cases."

A FAMILY AFFAIR

Over 50 years ago, at a little after 6 p.m. on the night of March 5, 1930, someone activated firebox 566 at the corner of Dundas and McCaul Streets here in Toronto. The person who sent in the alarm was never identified, and probably had no way of knowing that they were opening the curtain on one of Canada's most baffling murder cases.

Within minutes fire companies from Adelaide, Queen, and College Streets were dispatched to Goldberg Bros. Monument Works at 153 St. Patrick St. Firemen burst into the premises and quickly extinguished the flames. Fireman James Ridout was groping in the darkness, trying to find his way back to the door when his hand fell on something peculiar. He directed the beam of his small flashlight to the object and quickly realized that he had come upon the body of a man slumped over a desk. The upper portion of the body had been terribly burned with the face charred beyond recognition.

In this manner James Ridout found the body of Samuel Goldberg, 35, who was part owner of the monument firm. An autopsy performed on Goldberg revealed that a bullet had gone completely through his head. No weapon of any kind was found at the scene, but a small tin containing coal oil and a larger can of motor oil were found on the floor near the desk. Goldberg's clothing had been soaked in the oil.

The police, acting swiftly and efficiently, questioned friends and relatives of the deceased. Goldberg's wife, Sala, now a widow with two children; Norma, three; and Nathan. 21 months, could shed no light on the tragedy which had befallen her. Goldberg's partners in the monument business were his two brothers Harry and Abe, and his uncle, Abraham Steinberg. Harry and Abe were both absent from the

70

company offices that day and were never suspected of having caused the tragedy.

Abe Steinberg said that he had left the company office at 5 p.m., and was considered by the police to be the last person to see Sam alive. Because of this the police questioned Steinberg extensively for three hours, and finally arrested him on a holding charge of vagrancy.

Bits and pieces of information were uncovered during the police's preliminary investigation. Goldberg, who neither smoked nor drank, was shot at close range. A quantity of charred paper was found on top of Goldberg's desk. The fire had been confined to the area surrounding the desk. No fingerprints were found anywhere near the body.

In the meantime Abe Steinberg was released on bail of $5,000. Then, on March 7, two days after the murder, Det. Sgt. Arthur Levitt found a revolver while sifting through rubbish at the rear of Goldberg's office. The .38 calibre Colt had not been tossed away. It had been carefully placed under an old cement bag and pushed into the snow between a garage and a fence. The gun contained three fired and two live shells. Within days the police were able to trace the Canadian distributor of the U.S. manufactured weapon. The weapon had been sold on April 16, 1910, to the firm of Wood, Vallance & Co. in Hamilton. They in turn had sold it shortly after, but here the trail stopped. They could not trace the gun further.

The city of Toronto, and indeed most of Canada, was now humming with news of the mysterious murder of the mild mannered, respectable business man. Then, on March 25, Abraham Steinberg was charged with the murder of his nephew; a charge, which, if proven, carried an automatic death sentence.

The police revealed that a piece of lead had been found at the scene, and after the gun was located it was established that it had fired the fatal shot. An empty cartridge case from a .38 Colt revolver was found on a lot adjacent to the Goldberg property. Through the unglamorous task of sifting garbage and searching through snow, the detectives had uncovered the murder weapon, the lead slug and even the cartridge case.

The police were successful in finding young people who identified the murder weapon as belonging to Abe Steinberg.

It seems that two years previously Steinberg had owned a dry goods store in Chesley, Ont. Steinberg's son Phillip, had shown his father's gun to several friends. They now came forward to identify the gun. One youngster remembered that the gun had a chip out of its handle and picked the murder weapon from a row of nine guns.

The police also discovered that some money had been short in Steinberg's accounts with the firm. When asked by the other partners about this matter, Steinberg had come up with the missing money. Since the incident took place, the Goldberg brothers said things were never the same, and tensions ran high at the monument firm. They particularly emphasized the bad feeling between Steinberg and their murdered brother.

On Oct. 6, 1930, Abraham Steinberg stood trial for the murder of his nephew. During the trial it was revealed that when Steinberg's house was searched detectives had found overalls stained with human blood. Again the bad feeling between the accused and the murder victim was rehashed. In a sensational move, the Crown called one James Creighton who had spent time in the Don Jail with Steinberg. Creighton swore that Steinberg told him that he and Goldberg were always arguing. He also said Steinberg had told him that on the day of the murder he went to the monument works carrying a gun for protection. During a heated argument Steinberg had accidently killed Goldberg. Then he set the place on fire.

Rabbi Jacob Gordon told the strange story of a man who had knocked on his door at about 6 o'clock on the evening of the tragedy. The unknown man requested that the rabbi use his influence to prevent an autopsy being performed on Goldberg's body. The rabbi explained to the jury that religious custom prohibited a body from being cut. The visitor told the rabbi that there had been a fire at Goldberg Bros. and that Sam Goldberg had been burned to death. The rabbi had explained to the visitor that there was no way that he could prevent an autopsy if it was required and was the law of the land. The prosecution hinted strongly that Steinberg may have been the rabbi's visitor.

In Steinberg's defense, his wife took the stand and swore that the overalls found in their home did not belong to her husband. She said he had never worn nor owned a pair of overalls in his life. Defense attorneys admitted to the bad feeling between Steinberg and Goldberg, but put forth the rather plausible argument that disagreements between partners were a common occurrence and did not necessarily lead to murder. The defense also tried to discredit the Creighton story, and hinted of favors given in return for the co-operation of the witness. Lastly Rabbi Gordon emphatically stated that due to being nearsighted he could not identify Steinberg as the man who had the strange visit with him.

On Oct. 10, 1930, after four hours of deliberation, the jury failed to agree on a verdict and was dismissed. Steinberg stood trial for murder a second time on Feb. 1, 1931. This time the defense came up with several witnesses who testified that Steinberg was in Max Rotenberg's store between 5:10 p.m. and 7 p.m. on the night of the killing and could not have been the murderer. Countering this evidence was that of youthful Max Milgram, who swore he saw Steinberg in the vicinity of the fire between 6:30 and 7:45 p.m.

Steinberg was found guilty and was later sentenced to be hanged on April 21, 1931. His lawyer lodged an appeal and was turned down. A second appeal to the Supreme Court of Canada was lodged. As a result of this move, a stay of execution was granted so that the appeal could be heard. The Supreme Court dismissed the appeal, and a new execution date of July 14, 1931 was set. Despite a petition containing 40,000 signatures pleading for Steinberg's life, the federal cabinet denied clemency, and in their official jargon stated that "there be no interference with the death penalty".

As the execution date approached, Steinberg maintained his innocence. His religious counsel, Rabbi Samuel Sachs, disclosed that Steinberg never veered from his claim of innocence.

On July 14, at exactly 8 a.m. Steinberg was hanged for the murder of his nephew. A clock in the Steinberg home which had not chimed for over a year, rang out the hour at precisely 8 a.m. on that fateful day.

All that day Rabbi Sachs desperately tried to find a synagogue or fraternal organization to accept Steinberg's body. None would, and in the end Abraham Steinberg, draped in the prayer shawl which had been given to him as a boy in Poland, was laid to rest in a potter's field.

STRANGLER NELSON

The Boston Strangler managed to kill and mutilate 13 innocent women, terrorizing the city of Boston for several years.
Albert DeSalvo confessed to being the strangler, and was
committed to an institution. He had terrorized an entire city
to such an extent that women feared to walk the streets
alone.

Way back in 1927 Earle Nelson operated in much the
same manner as DeSalvo, except that he killed more fre-
quently and moved from city to city. He cut a swath of rape
and murder across the United States and into Canada.

Everyone who has researched the Nelson case agrees on
one thing—Earle Nelson was not normal. The best docu-
mented portion of his life began when he crossed the border
from the U.S. into Canada.

William Patterson worked in a Winnipeg department
store. He and his wife lived at 100 Riverton St. The couple
planned to sell their home, so while Bill Patterson was at
work his wife showed prospective buyers through the house.
To attract potential purchasers, they had placed a "For Sale"
sign prominently in a front window.

On a bright June day in 1927 Bill came home from work
and was startled to find that his wife was not at home. His
two children had spent the afternoon playing in a neighbor's
back yard. Patterson couldn't believe that his wife would
leave the children unattended. He phoned the police and
reported his wife missing.

In the meantime, despite his concern, Patterson had the
practical problem of caring for his two children. He prepared
the youngsters for bed. Later, in his own bedroom, he noticed that someone had forced open a suitcase in which he
and his wife kept their savings. When Patterson kneeled

down to take a closer look, he caught sight of his wife's coat under the bed. When he extended his arm, reaching for the coat, his hand came to rest on the neck of his dead wife.

The distraught man raced to a neighbor's house, blurted out the story of his tragic find and collapsed. The police were at the scene in a matter of minutes. Near Mrs. Patterson's body they found an old blue jacket and a pair of cheap cotton pants which did not belong to Mr. Patterson.

One of Patterson's brown suits was missing, along with $70 from the suitcase. It was obvious that the killer had left his old clothing at the scene of the murder, having first changed into Mr. Patterson's suit.

In the pockets of the cotton pants the police found newspaper clippings of rooms to let in Winnipeg. An examination of Mrs. Patterson's body revealed that she had been raped and strangled. The police recognized the similarity between this crime and those being committed by a monster who was roaming through the U.S., raping and murdering as he went. The "For Sale" sign, the woman alone, the rape, strangulation and theft, all pointed to the same man.

Was it possible that the man known as "The Strangler", or "The Gorilla Man" was in Winnipeg? The answer soon became apparent. So sure were the police that they had one of the most notorious killers in history among them that they commenced to canvass every home in Winnipeg advertising a room for rent on the chance that they might come up with the killer.

On the day following the murder the police found Mr. Patterson's brown suit in a pawnshop. In its pockets they found his cigarette lighter. The pawnshop proprietor distinctly remembered the man who had left the suit. He was an excellent customer. He had purchased an entire new outfit consisting of a light gray suit and overcoat. The customer had then asked the pawnshop owner for the location of a good barber. The merchant had accompanied the man to his own barber. The stranger had laughed and joked with the barber while in the shop. It is estimated that he had killed Mrs. Patterson only hours before.

A full description of the wanted man was sent to every law enforcement agency in the U.S. and Canada. By June 11 the strangler had managed to hitchhike to Regina, where he rented a room under the name Harry Harcourt. He was shocked to find his description all over the front pages of the Regina newspapers. In order to change his appearance once more he bought old workclothes at a local pawnshop, and by June 13 left Regina on foot.

Back in Winnipeg, a second body was discovered. Lola Cowan, a 14-year-old schoolgirl, had been enticed to her killer's room on the promise that he would purchase some flowers the girl was selling. Lola was contributing to her family's income by selling flowers after school. When her body was found under a bed it was obvious that she had been sexually attacked and strangled. The strangler had skipped out of his room on June 9 without paying his rent.

With the news of the discovery of the second victim the entire west was in a state of fear. Citizens bolted their doors and peered suspiciously at strangers from behind closed drapes. A living fiend was in their midst.

Although a complete description of the killer was widely distributed, and he had left a hot trail, it wasn't until Wednesday, June 15 that he was spotted. Leslie Morgan owned and operated a general store in Wakopa, Man., a tiny community of six houses about 250 miles southeast of Regina and 16 miles southwest of Killarney. Morgan served a soft drink and some cookies to a stranger. He was sure he had just served the strangler, and informed the Manitoba Provincial Police in Killarney. The police caught up with the fugitive a few miles south of Wakopa. He was arrested without incident and taken to Killarney. At 10:40 p.m. he was placed in jail. It took him exactly 20 minutes to pick the locks on his cell door and escape.

Nelson made his way to the Killarney railway station, figuring that he might be able to hop a train. He remained hidden until 8:10 a.m. when he came out of hiding in order to board an incoming train. He had no way of knowing it was a special train loaded down with police arriving expressly to take part in the manhunt. Nelson was quickly apprehended, handcuffed, and escorted to Winnipeg under heavy guard.

Who was Earle Nelson and what terrible crimes had he committed which made him the most hunted man in two countries?

Earle Nelson was born in San Francisco on May 12, 1897.

He attended school for a short time, but dropped out to become a transient laborer. By 1921 he had twice been confined to an insane asylum in California. After his second release Nelson married. His wife soon began to notice his childlike behavior. In fact, Nelson liked to play with children, and got along well with them. He would wander away from his wife and home for weeks at a time. When he returned he would behave as if he had been absent for only a few minutes. Finally, because of his erratic behavior, his wife had him confined for a third time. He escaped from the institution and was never recaptured.

When Nelson was safely behind bars in Winnipeg, police officials from a score of U.S. cities requested his fingerprints so they could be matched up with prints left at the scene of similar crimes in their cities. From these fingerprints and eyewitness reports, Nelson's path of terror was traced.

It is believed that he started killing on Feb. 20, 1926 in San Francisco. In succession he went to San Jose, returned to San Francisco, then on to Santa Barbara and Oakland. In all, five women were killed between Feb. 20 and Aug. 16, a period of just under six months. Nelson then struck in Portland, Oregon, where he strangled three women in three days. He travelled back to San Francisco, on to Seattle, Wash., returning to Portland, Ore. Nelson travelled continually throughout the winter of 1926-27. He strangled a woman in Council Bluffs, Iowa, and killed two women and a baby in Kansas City, Missouri.

In 1927, killing as he went, Nelson struck in Philadelphia, Buffalo, twice in Detroit, and in Chicago. From Chicago he travelled to Winnipeg where Mrs. Patterson and Lola Cowan became victims number 21 and 22. It is difficult to pinpoint the exact number of the strangler's victims, as it is believed that he may have killed more women whose murders, for one reason or another, were not attributed to him.

Earle Nelson did not look or act like a gorilla. All through his trial, which was held in Winnipeg on Nov. 1, 1927, he was mild mannered and polite to everyone who came in contact with him. His rather pleasant disposition had been used many times before to put unsuspecting women at ease. While posing as a prospective roomer he would always impress his potential victims with his polite chatter about church affairs. Many women who managed not to become victims came forward at the trial to testify how Earle Nelson had impressed them.

His trial was probably the most sensational ever held in Winnipeg. The courtroom was jammed, and thousands could not gain entrance to the courthouse. Nelson's wife and aunt were on hand to testify to Nelson's insanity in an attempt to save his life. Throughout it all Nelson remained composed and swore he never killed anyone. The evidence against him was overwhelming and he was found guilty.

On a chill January morning at daybreak Father J. A. Webb of St. Mary's Cathedral administered the last rites of the Catholic Church to Nelson. At precisely 7:41 a.m. his body plunged through the trap door of the gallows. Earle Nelson was 30-years-old. The date was Friday, Jan. 13, 1928.

THE DOCTOR WAS A KILLER

Not that much exciting happens in Brighton, Ont. Located 100 miles east of Toronto, a superhighway now bypasses the town, and only a green sign marks the direction to the quiet peaceful little community. Before the highway was built you had to go through Brighton. Years ago, in horse and buggy days, it was a main stopover point to rest up before hitting the big city.

Murder most foul is committed every day in all parts of the world, but very few contain ingredients to intrigue an entire country. More than 100 years ago the tiny community of Brighton was the unlikely setting for such a murder.

Ah, but let's start at the beginning.

Billy King was born in 1833 on a farm just outside Brighton. He was a bright and ambitious lad who yearned for knowledge and didn't mind applying himself. By 1855 he had finished normal school in Toronto and returned home as a full fledged teacher.

Now Billy had other, quite different yearnings, and it was somewhat of a surprise to the locals when our handsome hero started to court Sarah Lawson. Sarah left quite a bit to be desired in the looks department. She wore a perpetual frown, which gave her a rather stern appearance. Her personality was diametrically opposite to what one would describe as warm. Not only that, Sarah was flat chested. The powers that be have a way of evening things out. Sarah's father was loaded.

I can imagine the ladies of Brighton gossiping in the yard goods store over a bolt of gingham—"That handsome King boy is after the Lawson money."

Sure enough, handsome Billy married ugly Sarah, and received a veritable fortune of $10,000 in cold, hard cash.

79

The happy couple moved to Toronto, where a year later Sarah gave birth to a child. The baby died, and soon after this unfortunate occurrence the Kings started to bicker. Then they started to argue violently until Sarah did what so many ladies have done before and since. She went home to mother.

Thus unburdened, Billy threw himself into a new career, that of medicine. He enrolled in a medical college in Philadelphia and graduated as a bona fide medical doctor in 1858. He returned to his home town of Brighton and put out his shingle. Soon the wife and Billy reached a reconciliation. Dr. King's practice prospered. Past differences were forgiven and forgotten. Everything was coming up roses until the fall of 1858. Actually it was exactly Sept. 23, when the bloom came off the roses and love flew out the window, for on that day Billy King first laid eyes on Melinda Vandervoort.

Well, folks, where Sarah was flat, Melinda was well endowed. While Sarah's countenance was a perpetual frown, Melinda wore a smile. Dr. King was introduced to Melinda by his wife, which ended up being the biggest mistake she ever made. Melinda flirted with the smitten doctor at their very first meeting. The following day she again showed up at the King residence, and this time the pair found themselves alone. According to future revelations, they embraced vigorously during this second meeting. It has even been suggested that Melinda told Mrs. King that she was mad about Billy and intended to have him for herself.

Sarah knew of Melinda's checkered past. Melinda had a reputation as a homebreaker and was rather notorious for stealing other women's men. Sarah warned Billy, who told her she was silly for thinking such a thing.

Within a month Billy and Melinda were together constantly. Sarah was totally neglected. It is difficult to ascertain just exactly when Billy decided to murder his wife. From letters written to Melinda it is obvious that she would not consent to anything more intimate than a kiss from her lover. But she did offer much much more if only tiresome, flat chested Sarah was out of the way, and they were free to marry.

Sarah became ill. She constantly complained of stomach cramps. She was nauseous and lethargic. Her husband, being a man of medicine, tended to her every need. When, of necessity, the good doctor had to make house calls, kindly Melinda cared for the stricken woman. Despite all this loving attention, Sarah's condition deteriorated. On Nov. 4, 1858, Sarah died.

Sarah's parents never did care for their son-in-law. Now that the worst had happened, they decided to find out once and for all if their suspicions were based on fact. While Dr. King was out of his house, Mrs. Lawson searched the premises. She came up with incriminating letters from Melinda written to Billy, insinuating how convenient it would be to have Sarah out of the way. The Lawsons demanded an inquest into their daughter's death.

You can imagine the speculation in old Brighton town during the fall and early winter of '58. The frost lay heavy on the pumpkin, the cold winter winds blew, but who cared —did you hear "Dr. King may have done in his missus!"

Melinda thought it most prudent to visit relatives in Cleveland until things cooled off in once peaceful Brighton. Mrs. King's body was exhumed. It was found to contain arsenic. When the authorities went to arrest Dr. King they found that he thought discretion the better part of valor. Billy had skipped to Cape Vincent, on the U.S. side of Lake Ontario. The love crazed doctor was trying to make his way to Melinda's side in Cleveland when he was finally apprehended.

Dr. King was brought back to Canada to stand trial for murder. His trial began on April 4, 1859 at Cobourg. Sarah's parents testified to having seen Dr. King administer a white powder to their daughter which could have been arsenic.

Melinda caused a ripple through the courtroom when she denied ever having had designs on the medic. Fickle Melinda admitted that she had found a new flame in Cleveland, and was no longer interested in the hapless Billy. In fact, the voluptuous one went so far as to say that if the doctor was guilty he should be punished.

The jury agreed. They found Billy guilty and sentenced him to hang. After he was convicted, Dr. King confessed to murder. He claimed that he never administered arsenic to his wife, and had no idea how it had entered her body. He stated that he killed his wife with chloroform.

It matters little. On the morning of June 9, 1859, a huge crowd of over 7,000 gathered at Cobourg to witness Dr. King's hanging.

Whatever happened to Melinda? She never did marry her new beau from Cleveland. She gave him the same treatment she had given Dr. King. She then took up with another gentleman, who for a change, left her high and dry in Montreal. Melinda returned to Brighton, where she lived for many years, an object of scorn to many of the residents who knew her story. She took to drinking heavily, and died in the late 1890's, penniless and alone in an asylum in Toronto.

THE MAD TRAPPER OF RAT RIVER

"There I was around the bend. I got down on one knee, took careful aim with my .303 and squeezed the trigger. The mad trapper was trying to scramble up the banks of the frozen creek. My first shot sent him tumbling down, but didn't penetrate his pack. A second shot had the same effect. Then he turned, and without taking real aim, fired his 30 – 30 Savage. The impact of the bullet sent me sprawling."

I sat across the desk in Barrie, Ont. facing Earl Hersey, who was relating this tale of long ago when he was involved in what may have been Canada's greatest manhunt ever. If you are over 60 the story may bring back memories of below zero temperatures, dog teams, and the Arctic Circle, for in 1931-32 the Mad Trapper of Rat River was the main running news story in North America.

It all began innocently enough. The Royal Canadian Mounted Police were the only real law in the Northwest Territories and the Yukon. A part of the Mounties normal routine was to periodically check up on trappers and prospectors during weeks and even months of living in isolation. The world depression had drawn many an inexperienced man to the north country, ill equipped to withstand the hardships of that cold, barren land. Many of these men owe their lives to the R.C.M.P.

Const. Spike Millen of the Mounties' Arctic Red River Detachment first met Albert Johnson by chance in a store at Fort McPherson. He cautioned him that trapping in the area required a license. Johnson headed north and built a cabin near Rat River for the winter trapping season. The location of Johnson's cabin was close by the trapping lines of three native men, William Vittrekwa, William Nerysoo, and Jacob Drymeat.

Everyone who came into contact with Johnson described him in the same way. Evidently he was a close mouthed, rough man, who spoke with a slight Scandinavian accent. At the time of his appearance in the Arctic he was between 35- and 40-years-old, about 5 ft. 9 ins. tall, and of average build. It should be pointed out that, although living in isolation had its effect on many men, most were a gregarious lot who welcomed strangers. This was not the case with Johnson.

On Christmas Day, 1931, William Nerysoo entered the Mounties' quarters at the Arctic Red River Detachment. He told Const. Spike Millen that Johnson had sprung his traps and hung them on trees. It was decided that Const. Alfred "Buns" King and Special Const. Joe Bernard travel to Rat River to question Johnson.

Travelling by dog team through bitter cold, the men made the 25 mile trip in under two days. King approached Johnson's cabin. All seemed in order. Smoke was lazily drifting out of the chimney. King shouted, then pounded on the door of the cabin, but received no response, although he was certain that Albert Johnson was inside.

King decided that rather than force himself upon Johnson he should report the strange incident to his superior, Inspector Eames, Commander of the Mounties' subdivision at Aklavik. He and Bernard covered the 80 miles to Aklavik in two days hard travelling. Together with Const. R. G. McDowell and Special Const. Lazarus Sittichinli, they headed back to Johnson's cabin. There was some urgency as all the men wanted to celebrate New Year's Eve at Fort McPherson.

Again King approached the cabin. This time a shot pierced the still Arctic air. King was hit, but managed to crawl to safety. Johnson shot continuously from the cabin, while the Mounties returned his fire.

The three Mounties lashed the badly wounded King to a dogsled and set out on the 80 mile return trip. Their dogs had just made the trip to Johnson's cabin and were fatigued. The wind chill factor was equivalent to 90 degrees below zero. The terrain was rough and dangerous. The Mounties took only 20 hours to cover the 80 miles. The mad dash over the ice and snow certainly saved King's life. Johnson's bullet had gone clean through King's side. He recovered within a month.

Johnson's status had abruptly changed. He was no longer

a reticent troublemaker. He had fired at and wounded a member of the R.C.M.P.

Insp. Eames headed a party of nine men to bring in Johnson. Among these men was Const. Millen, the only one who had actually met the wanted man. On Jan. 9, 1932, the posse approached Johnson's cabin. No one expected him to be there, but strangely enough, Johnson had not moved. Insp. Eames coaxed Johnson to give up, explaining that King was going to survive. Nothing worked. Johnson responded by opening fire on the Mounties. He had dug a pit within the cabin. It was virtually impossible to hit the fugitive with gunfire.

The Mounties were not in that good a position. Their adversary was warm inside the cabin. They were exposed to the elements, and the longer they stayed the more food their dogs consumed. Further delay would see the party short of dog food.

Eames had brought dynamite along for just such a contingency. Dynamite sticks were tossed at the cabin, but they proved to be ineffective. Finally, one landed on the roof and blew a portion away, but this did not bother Johnson, who continued firing. In desperation several sticks of dynamite were fastened together and tossed at the cabin. The walls caved in, but still Johnson returned the Mounties fire. The battle had raged for almost a full 24 hours when Insp. Eames decided to return to Aklavik.

One man had held off a posse of nine well equipped Mounties and trappers, all experienced men of the North. Word drifted down from the Northland. The Mad Trapper of Rat River was still at large. One man against the combined strength of the R.C.M.P. and the elements. Everything possible, including dynamite, had been used to bring him in, but all had failed. It was quite a story. The hunt was a welcome diversion from the depression which gripped the world. Radio sales throughout North American increased dramatically expressly to hear news of the Mad Trapper of Rat River.

From Jan. 16 to Jan. 29, a large posse under Insp. Eames hunted the wanted man. Often they would pick up his trail, but each time he would manage to elude his hunters. Even his pursuers began to admire his resourcefulness and stamina against impossible odds.

On the 29th of January a portion of the posse, four men in

all, led by Spike Millen, found Johnson's camp. They waited until he was exposed beside a steep incline, but just as they were about to warn the surrounded man, Johnson spotted Millen. In an instant his 30-30 flashed into action. Millen and his companions returned the fire. During a lull in the shooting Millen shouted to the wanted man to surrender. The wind swirled in the still quiet that sometimes accompanies the bitter cold. The Mad Trapper, hunched behind a fallen log, remained silent.

Two hours passed. It was very possible Johnson was dead. Millen decided to take his man. Exposing himself, he walked forward a few paces. A shot whistled by Millen's ear as he lunged for cover. Johnson was alive. Millen returned his fire. The Mad Trapper shot once more, Millen sprang to his feet and collapsed in the snow. He was dead.

During the night Johnson scaled a cliff and escaped. Now Albert Johnson, the Mad Trapper of Rat River, was a murderer.

The Mounties brought their dead colleague back to Aklavik. Here Inspector Eames, who had great respect for the cunning of his adversary, regrouped his forces. For the first time in Canada, an airplane was employed in a manhunt. The plane's main function, other than to search for signs of the Mad Trapper, was to supply Eames' dogs with food. Previously searches had to be culminated as dog food ran low.

On Feb. 5, famed bush pilot Wop May joined the hunt.

Inspector Eames and his party, being supplied by May and his Bellanca, could now extend their search area.

In 1930, Staff Sgt. Earl Hersey had been sent to Herschel Island to open and maintain a radio station. In the winter he made his quarters in Aklavik. Hersey was only 18-years-old. He and a colleague, Sgt. Riddell, had been loaned by the Army Signal Corps to the Mounties. Hersey knew more than radio. A crack shot, the young, tough sergeant was an expert with dogs and sled.

During the first week in February, Albert Johnson, now a rag tag desperate man who had lived off the barren land for over a month, made a break for freedom. During a raging blizzard he managed to cross the treacherous Richardson Mountains. He was spotted near Eagle River. On Feb. 13, thirteen men, trappers, Army personnel, and Mounties started off through the mountains via Rat Pass. Wop May in his Bellanca picked up Johnson's trail on Feb. 14, about 20 miles up the Eagle River.

Six dog teams followed Johnson's trail. The cunning Johnson was travelling in cariboo tracks in an attempt to evade detection. Young Sgt. Hersey, with his top notch team of dogs, led the hunt.

Years later, the 66-year-old Hersey describes the scene this way: "With six dog teams yelping and barking there was a lot of noise. We were travelling up the bed of a creek when I came to a hairpin turn. Later we all realized what happened. Johnson, out of sight around the bend, heard our noise and thought we were coming from the other direction. We spotted each other at approximately the same time. We were heading toward each other at a distance of about 300 yards. That's when the shooting started."

When the shot tore into Hersey's knee, elbow and side he dropped immediately into the soft snow. Hersey was paralyzed from the waist down, but had full use of his arms. He frantically burrowed as fast as he could in the snow. The Mad Trapper fired three more shots at Hersey, but all missed their target.

By this time the other dog teams appeared on the scene. Johnson ignored the Mounties' warning shout. A fusillade of bullets brought the wanted man down. His body had been hit by 17 bullets. The Mad Trapper of Rat River was dead.

Wop May, who was observing the shootout from the air, brought his Bellanca to rest beside the seriously wounded Hersey. In less than an hour the wounded man was in a hospital in Aklavik. Throughout his ordeal he remained conscious and has total recall of the entire episode.

"My arm didn't hurt much, nor did the hole in my side, but my knee hurt like hell."

All Hersey's wounds were tended without the use of anesthetic. Later, Hersey noted a wrinkle on his bedsheet. He patted the wrinkle, but it wouldn't go away. A nurse mentioned the incident to a doctor, who examined the area. He found that a bullet had travelled clear through Hersey's side and had lodged about a quarter of an inch under his skin. The doctor cut the skin and presented Hersey with the bullet, which he has to this day.

Although there have been many theories about Johnson's

life before he entered the Arctic, no one has succeeded in positively identifying him. He simply appeared in the North country as a quiet, gruff man with no past.

Sgt. Hersey continued in the Army until retiring in 1954 with the rank of Major. Today he devotes much time to Red Cross work. Almost all traces of the great manhunt have slowly disappeared. Hersey's mitts and parka are on display beside Johnson's homemade snowshoes in the R.C.M.P. Museum in Regina.

The Mad Trapper of Rat River has left one lasting memorial. Picking up a broom handle, Earl Hersey is quick to point out, "That bullet hole through the elbow has affected my golf swing to this day."

SLAUGHTER AT SHELL LAKE

Murder is the most reprehensible and horrendous crime that man can inflict on his fellow man. The motives which generate this most final of all acts can come from a variety of sources—greed, hate, lust, jealousy; the list is endless. But what of the murders which take place without motive, without reason and without explanation? Nothing can be more tragic. This is the story of one such murder.

Shell Lake, Saskatchewan is a tiny farming community of 250 people, situated about 90 miles north west of Saskatoon. The closest town of any size is Prince Albert. The huge farms often associated with western Canada are not evident in this area. The farms are small. Hardy men work long, hard hours in the fields to wrest a living from the ground. In addition to their crops, they raise horses, cattle, pigs and chickens.

Jim Peterson had a farm about four miles from Shell Lake. Jim's farm was about a mile square, and stood about 300 yards off Highway 3. A plain clapboard farm house was home to 47-year-old Jim, his 42-year-old wife, Evelyn, and their eight children, ranging in age from Larry, 1, to Jean, 17. An older daughter, Katherine, had recently married and was living in Chetwynd, B.C.

Wildrew Lang owned the farm adjoining the Peterson's. Lang and Peterson often worked together on each other's farms. During haying time they pooled their labor, first doing one farm and then the other.

At 8:30 on the morning of Aug. 15, 1967, Wildrew Lang started off in his truck for the Peterson farm. Because the men were always giving each other a helping hand, they rarely drove down their long driveways and along Highway 3 to the next farm. Instead they had worn a sort of path or crude road through a connecting field in order to go directly from one farm to another.

On this perfect summer day, Lang and Peterson were going to clean out a granary, which was really an old house used for storage. It was located not too far from the Peterson house. Lang made his way across the field and started to load his truck alone. He idly thought that Jim should have joined him. They had discussed loading the grain the night before. Jim planned on hauling it to the elevator, so that he could give his 17-year-old daughter, Jean, a little extra money. Jean was a runner, and was soon to take part in a track and field meet in Dundurn, Sask. The whole Peterson family was excited about the prospect of Jean running.

What could be keeping Jim? Lang decided to go to the farmhouse and find out. As he approached the front door it dawned on him that it seemed to be so very quiet and still. It was close to 9 o'clock. Where was Jim? Eight active kids, and not a sound to be heard.

Lang opened the door and apprehensively called out, "Hello." He peered inside. There, on the kitchen floor, clad only in his shorts, lying face down, was the body of his friend, Jim Peterson. Lang didn't look any further. He drove the few miles to Shell Lake and made contact with the R.C.M.P. at Spiritwood.

Cpl. B. L. Richards arrived at the Peterson home, and while Lang waited in the car outside, Cpl. Richards entered the house. He instinctively knew that Jim Peterson was dead. In the living room, on a cot, he found the body of 11-year-old Dorothy. He continued on to the children's bedroom. In the first bed he discovered the bodies of Pearl, 9, and Jean, 17. In another double bed were three bodies—Mary, 13; William, 5; and Colin, 2. All had been shot in the head.

Cpl. Richards noticed a slight movement between the bodies of Pearl and Jean. He bent over and discovered tiny 4-year-old Phyllis, her face buried in her mattress. Richards lifted her from the bed and took her outside. The child didn't speak. Richards saw to it that she was taken to a farm across the highway.

Cpl. Richards then drove to Shell Lake for help. He returned accompanied by Dr. J. R. Michaud. As he approached the house for the second time he discovered the bodies of Mrs. Peterson and baby Larry, clad only in his diaper. The bodies were found outside the house. Mrs. Peterson had grabbed her infant son and jumped out a window in an attempt to escape. Both had been shot through the head.

Nine human beings had fallen that morning to some madman. Who could hate this God fearing, hard working family enough to kill them? Why the Petersons? Why was Phyllis spared?

The R.C.M.P. had no murder weapon and no motive, but they did have some clues. The killer had left an identifiable footprint on the Peterson's kitchen floor. It had been made by a rubber boot, which had distinguishable markings. One of these markings were the words "Made in Taiwan". The bullets which had killed the Petersons came from a .22 calibre rifle.

Three days after the murder the R.C.M.P. received a call from a farmer. He gave them the name of someone whom he thought they should check out. The name was Victor Hoffman.

Victor was 21-years-old. He had been in and out of trouble for the past few years. From 1961 to 1964 he had been charged three times with breaking and entering. Each time it appeared that he was interested in stealing guns. He had received a two-year suspended sentence for these offences. More recently he had behaved strangely around his own home. When he started shooting his rifle in the air, explaining that he was shooting at the devil, his parents had him committed to the Saskatchewan Mental Hospital at North Battleford.

While being treated at the hospital he confessed to doctors that he had seen the devil many times. From as far back as he could remember the devil had appeared to him. He described the apparition as being well over six feet tall with a face resembling a pig's. Doctors in the mental institution diagnosed Victor's illness as schizophrenia. They prescribed drugs to suppress his hallucinations, as well as electric shock treatments.

Victor received a series of 12 shock treatments, and seemed to improve. On July 26th he was released. While still introverted, he was capable of working on the farm and socializing with acquaintances. The doctors who released him felt that drugs would keep his illness under control.

The R.C.M.P. visited the Hoffman farm, and confiscated

Victor's .22 calibre Browning rifle and his rubber boots. On Aug. 19, four days after the murders, and the day of the Petersons' funeral, the Crime Detection Laboratory in Regina informed the investigating officers that Victor Hoffman's rubber boots had made the track on the Petersons' kitchen floor, and his rifle had fired all the fatal bullets.

Victor Hoffman was taken into custody and questioned. He told the police that on Aug. 15 he got out of bed at 4 a.m. and worked on the family car. Then, without warning, Victor blurted out, "O.K., I killed them. I tried to change the rifling on it. I should have burned the house, then you would not have found those cartridges. I stopped at the gate. I don't know what made me do it. I collected 17 cartridges. I didn't want to shoot any more. The one I left didn't see me."

When Victor's rifle was examined it showed signs of having been tampered with in order to make ballistic comparisons more difficult. In his original statement above, and later, Hoffman was obsessed with changing the characteristics of his rifle so that the fatal bullets could not be traced back to him. His statement also revealed why little Phyllis was spared. She had not looked up, and in his warped mind Hoffman ordained that she would live because she could not identify him.

Victor was studied extensively by psychiatrists. His story began to unfold. After working on the car on the day of the murder, the devil told him to go for a drive. The thought entered his mind that he should kill both his parents, but instead he put a box of shells in the glove compartment, and placed his loaded .22 on the front seat. Victor took off, and as he passed each house he had an urge to pull into the driveway and kill the occupants. As he drove past each farm the urge grew stronger, until at last he did pull into a driveway. It was the farm of Jim and Evelyn Peterson.

Victor opened the front door. Jim Peterson was sitting on the side of his bed in his shorts and was about to put on his shoes. Jim looked up, saw the rifle, and lunged at Hoffman. Victor emptied his rifle at Jim, whose forward motion brought him almost to Hoffman's feet.

The children screamed. Hoffman went out to his car, reloaded his rifle and systematically went through the house, killing all the children. He killed Mrs. Peterson and the baby in the yard. They had made their way out through a window.

Little Phyllis was purposely left alive. Hoffman says it was because she didn't see him. Psychiatrists feel that the reason she was spared was because his impulse to kill was exhausted. Hoffman had never met nor even seen any member of the Peterson family until the August morning he opened their front door.

Victor Hoffman stood trial for murder and was found Not Guilty due to insanity. He was confined to a mental institution.

FUNERAL PYRE ON THE FARM

A Nazi concentration camp is an unlikely place for romance, but it was there in German occupied Poland that Isaac Wertman met Rywa, his future wife. After they were liberated, Isaac and Rywa were married in Warsaw. It is ironic that the couple, who managed to escape Hitler's gas ovens, was destined to become linked forever with a young Canadian boy whose father had served as a soldier in the German army before emigrating to Canada.

Isaac and Rywa arrived in Canada in 1951 and settled in Toronto. The years drifted by, and two children were born to the two survivors. Yet their marriage was not a happy one. Rywa craved the attention of other men, while Isaac strived to make a living in the garment industry. The Wertmans bought a home on Warwick Ave. Their two children grew up and left their parents' home. Later they were to state that their mother and father constantly bickered. Isaac, a less aggressive individual than his wife, usually received the worst of these exchanges. It became obvious that he knew his wife was seeing other men.

Toward the end of 1972 Isaac left his wife and moved into an apartment. He initiated divorce proceedings. His lawyer advised him that half the value of the Wertman home was rightfully his. Rywa was informed that the settlement amount would be $25,000. She was beside herself with anguish at giving up half the value of her home.

Besides, Rywa had taken a lover. Max Goldstein was now firmly esconced in the house on Warwick Ave. Posing as a roomer, it was a sort of open secret that Max was Rywa's lover and was footing some of the bills. In the meantime Rywa took a job as a dancing teacher. It was in this way that she met 22-year-old Manfred Baron.

It wasn't long before Rywa was teaching Manfred dancing, and other things as well. He moved into the house on Warwick Ave. The young man, who was less than half the age of his lover, fell hard for the older woman. Manfred had been brought up on a farm near Acton and had never met anyone as worldly and sophisticated as Rywa. Later it was revealed that the purpose of his dancing lessons had been an attempt to gain confidence with the opposite sex.

The entangled lives of all the principals in our cast might have untangled eventually had it not been for Rywa's obsessive fear of losing half her home to her estranged husband.

Isaac Wertman worked on Spadina Ave. for a clothing firm owned by Harry Patinek. Isaac always opened up in the morning. Harry was surprised when he arrived at his establishment on the morning of May 8, 1974 and found his employees waiting outside for the doors to be opened.

As a concerned employer, Harry called Isaac's apartment several times. When he received no answer, he went to the apartment, but Isaac was nowhere to be found. Harry noticed that Wertman's car was in the parking lot. He decided to call the police. When the officer arrived, he and Harry took a look at Isaac's car. They found blood on the bumper and bloodstains on the asphalt surrounding the front of the vehicle.

An investigation into the disappearance of Isaac Wertman was conducted by the police. Almost immediately their inquiries turned up incriminating evidence. Neighbors stated that they had heard screams and scuffling emanating from the parking lot where Wertman's car was found.

Within 10 days the police had an idea of the involved lives being led by Rywa Wertman and Manfred Baron. They approached Manfred at a construction site, and asked him about the missing Wertman. He surprised them by readily incriminating himself, revealing intimate facts about the case. He told the police officers that Isaac would never be found without his help. Then he took the total blame, saying that he had acted alone.

Manfred signed a detailed statement telling how he had waited for Isaac outside the latter's apartment building. He struck the older man over the head with a club, then shoved him into his car and drove to his father's farm near Acton. Isaac wasn't dead. When they arrived at the farm, Manfred hit his victim over the head again. Then he took Isaac out to the back field where there was a 45-gallon drum. He put the limp form in the drum and, using diesel fuel, managed in 15 hours to burn what had once been Isaac Wertman.

He later buried what remained of Isaac under some sod. When Manfred led the authorities to the drum, it had seven bullet holes in it which were never really explained. Manfred was placed in the Don Jail. He patiently waited for three weeks to receive help from his lover. When it didn't come he changed his story.

Now he involved his mistress. He claimed that he had only disposed of the body. He said Rywa had been there in the parking lot with him. She had killed her husband by shooting him with Manfred's .22 calibre revolver. Rywa had found out that very day that her husband definitely had a claim on her home, and talked Manfred into waiting for him in the parking lot.

The police then visited Rywa, who became almost incoherent when she heard that Manfred had changed his story. She accused her boyfriend of being the murderer. So we have the classic case which has been repeated so often, of lovers accusing each other of the actual act of murder.

A year later both Manfred and Rywa stood trial for conspiracy to commit murder. Conviction carried a sentence of 14 years imprisonment. Defended by separate lawyers, each accused the other of murder. It was indefinite whether Isaac had been clubbed to death or if he had been shot.

Dr. J. W. A. Duckworth gave the most hair raising evidence when he stated that Wertman's head had been cut off before it had been placed into the burning drum. He could not state with certainty if Wertman had been alive or dead when he was decapitated.

The defense pointed out that Rywa and Max Goldstein may have set up the naive Manfred to murder Isaac. In this way Rywa would not have to pay her husband the $25,000 settlement, and would be free to marry Goldstein.

There was also evidence that as soon as Isaac was out of the way, Goldstein, who was then still living with Rywa, moved out of the Warwick Ave. home. Manfred, who occupied the basement of the home, moved back to Acton.

It had been close to the perfect murder, for had Harry Patinek not called the police, who discovered the blood in the parking lot and on Isaac's bumper, it is quite possible the murder would have gone undetected.

The jury deliberated six hours and reported back to the court that they were deadlocked. The next day, after two further hours of deliberation, they brought back a verdict of guilty in both cases.

Both Manfred and Rywa received sentences of 14 years in prison. Both appealed this conviction, and had their convictions overturned. At his new trial Baron pleaded guilty, and received an 11-year prison sentence. Tried separately, Rywa was again found guilty, and this time received an 8-year prison sentence.

ACCUSED PRIEST

Over the years, Montreal has been the scene of many notorious murders. In recent years mobsters have perpetrated horrendous mass killings, but none of them compare to the sensation caused by the Father Delorme murder: This particular crime has the dubious distinction of being Montreal's, and quite possibly Canada's, most sensational murder.

It happened long ago, but is still recalled by old timers, who remember the headlines and speculation which kept the good citizens of La Belle Province talking about little else for almost three years. You see, the principal character, and the man who eventually stood trial for murder, not once, but three times, was a Roman Catholic priest. To my knowledge Father Adelard Delorme is the only priest who has ever stood trial for murder in Canada.

Early on Saturday morning, Jan. 7, 1922, James Higginbotham and Elric Larin trudged through the crisp Montreal snow toward a shack on the corner of Colebrook and Snowdon Streets. Both men worked for the city, and the shack contained their tools. As they walked, they caught sight of the crumpled form of a man lying in the snow. There was no doubt that he was dead. The man's overcoat was saturated with blood, as was a quilt-like material wrapped about his head.

The two city employees summoned the police, who were at the scene in a matter of minutes. Investigating officers noted that the snow under the body had not melted, indicating that the victim probably was dead and cold before being placed where he had been found. Upon searching the body the officers discovered letters addressed to Raoul Delorme, 190 St. Hubert St., Montreal.

The body was removed to the city morgue. The quilt-like

material was unwrapped from the head, revealing six bullet wounds. The victim's hands were securely tied together with cord. There were no bullet holes in his overcoat.

When officers called at 190 St. Hubert St., they encountered a Roman Catholic priest, Father Adelard Delorme. Police accompanied him to the morgue to view the body. Father Delorme tearfully and regretfully identified the victim as his half-brother, Raoul.

Father Delorme explained that his half-brother was a commerce student at the University of Ottawa, and was at home on vacation. The priest became enraged when he was informed that someone had bound his brother's hands and poured six bullets into his head at close range. Then the murderer must have pinned the overcoat over the head and transported the body to the field where it was found. What coldblooded madman would do such a thing to a 24-year-old student?

On Monday, Jan. 9, a coroner's inquest was conducted into the death of Raoul Delorme. Father Delorme was the principal witness. He explained his family's history.

Adelard Delorme's father had been a wealthy contractor who died leaving an estate of over $160,000. The estate, consisting mainly of several properties located in Montreal's east end, was left to six relatives. The largest portion by far had been left to Raoul, who received an income in excess of $10,000 per year from the properties.

Father Delorme administered his late father's estate, and took care of Raoul's income as well. In fact, Raoul was attending the University of Ottawa solely to become equipped in the ways of finance in order to handle his own affairs upon graduation.

At the inquest, some curiosity was expressed as to why Father Delorme did not have a regular parish. He readily disclosed the details. Delorme was born in Ste. Anne des Plaines, Que. After attending the village school, he entered Ste. Therese College, and then studied theology at Montreal's Grand Seminary on Sherbrooke St.

At the time of the murder he was 37-years-old, having been ordained for some years. Father Delorme had been appointed vicar of the Ste. Anne des Plaines Church in 1915, and later was transferred, again as vicar, to the church at Tetreaultville, near Montreal. This latter move had been made at his own request, as his father's death and his position as sole executor of the estate made it imperative for him to be located near Montreal.

Father Delorme explained that after a year he found he could not properly attend to the affairs of the parish as well as his father's estate. He requested special dispensation to change positions once more. Permission was granted, and he became chaplain of L'Assistance Publique. This enabled him to administer his father's estate.

On the evening of Jan. 6 Raoul phoned his brother from downtown Montreal. He informed Father Delorme that he was staying downtown for supper, and planned on visiting a theatre with friends. Raoul also mentioned that if he didn't return by 11:30 he would not be coming home that night. When, and if, he made that phone call, Raoul didn't realize that he only had hours to live.

Later that night Father Delorme stated that he had received several strange phone calls, with no one at the other end of the line. Once he thought he heard loud moaning. He claimed to have reported the incident to the phone company. Later, phone company officials stated that they had no record of his complaint.

Two days into the inquest, with detectives working around the clock checking out every possible clue, Father Delorme turned over a .25 calibre Bayard automatic revolver to them. He stated that he kept it in his car for protection. Normally he used his late father's old weapon but, by coincidence, a few days before the murder he had traded in his old weapon for his present one. Raoul had been shot with a .25 calibre weapon.

On Wednesday, Jan. 11 funeral services for Raoul Deforme were conducted at St. James Church in downtown Montreal. Father Delorme celebrated the requiem mass.

The Coroner's inquest was delayed several times in order to examine new evidence which was constantly being uncovered by the police. In the meantime, Father Delorme issued statements which were extremely newsworthy under the circumstances. Every word he uttered was conscientiously reported in the daily press.

A few days after the funeral Father Delorme announced that he was posting a $10,000 reward for the arrest and conviction of the murderer. He duly deposited this amount in the Bank of Hochelaga. Father Delorme was full of announcements. He also stated that once the murderer was convicted, he should be publicly executed at a local outdoor skating rink. Such proclamations were not becoming to a man of the cloth.

When it was learned that Father Delorme was the main beneficiary of Raoul's will, suspicion openly fell upon the priest. It seemed impossible, but as the days wore on, more and more circumstantial evidence pointed to Father Delorme as a murderer. It couldn't be. Nothing like this had ever happened in Montreal before. Saving souls, yes. Saving lives, yes. But a priest a murderer! There had to be some other explanation.

Father Delorme kept spewing quotable quotes. He likened himself to his Saviour, and compared the slanderous remarks made about him to those hurled at Jesus Christ during his last days on earth.

At precisely 7 p.m. on Feb. 14, 1922, Father Delorme was arrested and charged with the murder of his half-brother, Raoul Delorme.

The thought of a Roman Catholic priest standing trial for murder was so against the grain of the average Quebecker in 1922 that many thought it was all an English plot to undermine the church.

Those who remember the murder recall the unbelievable aspects of the case. The fact that the victim was bound and had been shot six times almost precluded the possibility that a priest could have been the perpetrator of such a horrendous act. Rumors of every kind spread throughout Montreal. Everyone had a pet theory. Newspaper circulation soared as the news spread through the province of Quebec and across the land. Word of a priest being tried for murder was reported in the press of Europe and even Asia.

Father Delorme's legal counsel pleaded that his client was insane, and therefore unfit to stand trial. For a while it appeared that this tactic would be successful, for on June 30 a special jury did find Father Delorme insane. He was committed to the Beauport Asylum. Almost a year later, in May, 1923, Father Delorme was released from the asylum on the grounds that he was now sane. The month following his release he was committed to trial for the murder of his brother. The trial began on June 20, 1923.

A tremendous amount of circumstantial evidence was presented in an effort to prove the priest guilty of murder. Motive was established when Monsignor Rheaume of Ottawa took the witness stand. He told of a day in February, 1921, when Raoul was to undergo a minor operation in Ottawa. On that occasion, Father Delorme and Raoul composed Raoul's will in longhand in the hospital. The Monsignor had signed it as a witness. Under the terms of the will Feather Delorme was to receive the bulk of Raoul's estate upon his death.

To add fuel to the fire, it was established that only seven days before the murder a $25,000 insurance policy had been issued on Raoul's life. Father Delorme was the sole beneficiary and had paid the first premium.

Because there were no bullet holes in the victim's overcoat, it had been theorized that Raoul had been shot indoors. Dr. Derome, who performed the autopsy, lent credence to this theory, when he testified that the piece of quilt wrapped around the dead man's head corresponded to quilting found in Father Delorme's home. Dr. Derome, who achieved star status during the trial, also testified that he had found bloodstains in the priest's car. Father Delorme claimed these stains were the result of the scratches to his knuckles received when he had changed a flat tire.

A gunsmith, Cesar Haynes, testified that he had sold Father Delorme a .25 calibre revolver only 10 days before the murder. Upon comparing a bullet extracted from Raoul's head with one fired from the priest's gun, the gunsmith was willing to state that both bullets had most probably come from the same gun.

Raoul's rubbers and overshoes were found at home. The Crown felt that he had been killed in the cellar of Father Delorme's home. They claimed it was quite possible that Father Delorme had planned to kill his brother with one shot at close range. Upon testing it was discovered that his revolver was constructed in such a way that the sight was off by one and three quarter inches. The initial bullet had travelled through the side of Raoul's face, rather than directly into his temple. They further claimed that once Father Delorme wounded his brother, he had no choice but to keep on shooting.

Every minute of the night of the murder came under close scrutiny. The house at 190 St. Hubert was home to Father Delorme, his three sisters, Lily, Rosa, and Florence, and, of course, Raoul, home from Ottawa on vacation.

All the occupants gave evidence that Raoul left the house after lunch, stating that he might not be back for supper. Lily and Florence had supper with Father Delorme. All three sisters left the house to attend the theatre about 8 o'clock that evening, and didn't return until 11:20 p.m.

At 8 o'clock Father Delorme went outdoors, where he was observed by several witnesses. He returned at 9:30. If Raoul was killed at home, Father Delorme was the only one there, and could have committed the crime between 9:30 and 11:20, when his sisters returned. Neighbors swore they heard Father Delorme's car at about 11 o'clock that night in the lane beside his garage. They heard the garage door open and close, but were unable to state if he was coming in or going out.

The victim's pocket watch had been torn from his body. A piece of watch chain was found hanging from his pocket. Strangely, the watch itself was anonymously sent by mail to Chief of Provincial Detectives Lorraine. The writing on the parcel containing the watch was carefully examined. Experts compared the handwriting on the parcel to that of Father Delorme. Three experts swore the writing matched that of Father Delorme, while a fourth refused to swear to it.

The Crown claimed that the priest had sent the watch as an erratic method of getting rid of it. The defense countered with the claim that someone had probably stumbled across the body and had stolen the watch. Later a guilty conscience may have forced them to mail the watch to the police.

Father Delorme stated simply that all the evidence against him was circumstantial. No one saw him kill his brother. He was in his cellar from about 10 o'clock that night until one in the morning repairing a furnace, until one of his sisters called out to him to come to bed.

The jury retired to reach a verdict. On July 21, they reported that they were hopelessly deadlocked. Sent back to continue their deliberations, they reported two days later that they stood at 10 for conviction and two for acquittal. They were dismissed.

The jury, made up of French and English citizens, were criticized for not bringing in a guilty verdict. It was believed that no one of the Catholic faith would find a priest guilty of murder. We must remember that a guilty verdict was tantamount to death on the gallows in 1923.

In February, 1924, Delorme's second trial for murder again resulted in a deadlocked jury. It all had to be done a third time.

Father Delorme's third and last murder trial began on Oct. 6, 1924, almost three years after his brother's body was found with six bullets in his head. On Oct. 31 the jury retired to reach a decision. Thousands stood outside the old courthouse awaiting the result of their deliberations. Three hours and forty five minutes later they returned with their verdict: Not Guilty.

Father Delorme made a brief statement: "I knew I would be freed," he stated, "because I am innocent. I hold no grudge against any person who worked against me in the case. I forgive all."

With that magnanimous statement he walked out of the courtroom a free man after spending more than two years and nine months in jail and asylums. The verdict was received outside the province of Quebec as a travesty of justice.

Father Delorme died of natural causes in 1942.

PART 3

THE CON ARTISTS

THE GOAT GLAND CAPER

Now that Toronto has the C.N. Tower, the tallest free standing building in the world, we citizens must be wary that some rascal doesn't sell it. In the world of swindlers and con men such a proposition is not altogether ridiculous. Over the years con men have sold the Brooklyn Bridge, Eiffel Tower, and one even rented out most of the State of Arizona.

Who was the most ridiculous con man of all time? Here is my nominee for champ: John Romulus Brinkley. You see, John didn't sell buildings or bridges. He sold something that man has been searching for through all recorded history—youth. For a price our hero would return the virility of youth. To use his own words, "You'll be back a kickin' and a scratchin' in no time."

In 1885 John first saw the light of day in Beta, a North Carolina hamlet of 200 dirt poor farmers. When John was six his mother died of tuberculosis. Four years later he lost his father to the same disease.

By the time John was 16 he had outgrown Beta. The grass looked so much greener in Baltimore that he decided to try his luck in the big city. Being smarter than most former citizens of Beta, John decided to start at the top. He applied for admission to Johns Hopkins Medical School. The dean of the school informed him that there were a few formalities which had to be complied with before he could be admitted to the famous university. There was the minor matter of a grade school education, not to mention a high school diploma.

John felt these prerequisites were totally unfair and unwarranted. He sought out a school where, for a price and a minimum of study, he could obtain a medical degree of sorts. Quick as a bunny, he managed to acquire one of these watered down degrees from the Eclectic Medical University of Kansas City. While he was at it he managed to woo and win Sally Wilkie, a fair damsel from his home state of North Carolina.

Armed with a degree in one hand and winsome Sally in the other, John set up his practice in Fulton, Kansas. Soon he and Sally were blessed with a baby daughter. After the birth of the child Sally found that she really wasn't crazy about John after all. In fact, when she thought about their relationship she discovered he was too despicable to live with. She asked him for a divorce, but John refused to give in to her demand.

Apparently Sally's affection for her husband could be turned on in fits and starts. In the next few years they had two more daughters, and again Sally approached John for a divorce. This time he said good riddance and granted the lady her freedom.

John's practice had never really flourished. In fact, it consisted mainly of selling patent medicines. In the summer of 1910, while visiting in Memphis, John met and married one Minnie Jones. Now that he again had female companionship, he looked around for a town where he could make a buck. He and Minnie picked Milford, Kansas, which had neither a doctor nor a hospital.

History is a little vague as to where John got the bright idea that the glands of a goat could be transplanted to male humans and rejuvenate their sexual drive and performance. The story goes that a farmer who had not been, shall we say, active for 16 long years, asked for the operation. John complied, and the following year the farmer's wife gave birth to a bouncing baby boy.

Say what you will about John Romulus Brinkley, he recognized a good thing when he saw it. He tried the operation on a few willing relatives, and soon word got around Kansas that there was a doctor named Brinkley who could restore love to your heart and put that old gleam back in your eye. John's practice mushroomed, so that the scallywag actually built a 50-room hospital to accommodate his patients. Naturally it was called the John Brinkley Hospital.

The patient entered John's hospital on Monday, had his goat gland operation, and was released on Friday, apparently full of vim, vigor and whatever. The one thing he didn't have on Friday was $750, because that was the exact amount John charged for his and the goat's services.

This was just great for the would be Kansas studs, but it didn't do a thing for the billy goats. In fact John was going through goats faster than Midas goes through mufflers. Soon the billy goat population of Kansas was drastically depleted. Undaunted John's agents spread out through Arkansas in their quest for billy goats.. In their wake they left an overabundance of widowed nanny goats, but then someone has to suffer in the interest of medical science.

Business became so lucrative that Doc Brinkley raised his price to $1,500 per operation. To give you an idea of the loot involved, Doc and his assistants were now performing 50 transplants per week.

There were a few practical problems. The railway had to build a new spur to Milford in order to take care of the goat supply being shipped into the town. Doc built a wing onto the hospital to house his staff of assistants and nurses.

Milford even had its own baseball team. They were aptly called the Brinkley Goats.

By 1922 radio was coming into its own, and John immediately realized that the newfangled instrument held tremendous possibilities. Not one to do things half way, he built his own station, KFKB in Milford. He started to advertise his gland operation and as a result had to double his hospital's capacity to accommodate 100 suckers per week.

John then stumbled on the idea of diagnosis by radio. The listener could write into KFKB and John would tell the sufferer what his or her trouble was and prescribe a remedy over the air. The idea was a hit. John produced the cures himself. Most of them consisted of different strength aspirin and Castor oil. The diagnosis-from-a-distance business became so popular that John designated a different number for the different strengths of his phony prescriptions: "Yes, Ma'am, Number 9 and Number 14 should fix you up in no time," his resonant voice would reassure the listeners of KFKB.

His program was called "Brinkley's Medical Question Box", and it became so popular that only the most interesting cases were answered on the air. An incredible 50,000 letters per day were arriving at KFKB by 1923. No kidding, they actually had to build a new post office in the town to handle the flow of cash pouring in.

John accumulated a few trinkets along the way. He now had a Cadillac, a Lincoln, his own airplane, two yachts, and diamond rings more numerous than fingers. He had come a long way from Beta, North Carolina.

In the background there were some faint rumblings. The American Medical Association took a dim view of the goat business, but that association was nowhere near the powerful body it is today and didn't do that much to slow John down. A man from New Jersey died of tetanus after being rejuvenated, but John bought his way out of that particular scrape.

One day while vacationing in Florida, John told his startled wife Minnie that he needed a diversion. He thought he would try politics. "By gosh," John said, "I'll run for the governorship of Kansas." The final candidacy filing date had passed, so John had to run as a write-in candidate. To vote for him, one actually had to write his name on the ballot. John campaigned with his airplane and his radio station. To give you an idea of his power and popularity, out of 617,369 votes cast for the three candidates, John came in third with 183,278 votes. The winner of the election won by a miniscule 251 votes over the second place finisher. John had really thrown a scare into the political machines of the state, and he had accomplished it all, virtually alone.

John went back to selling his medicine with a vengeance. He built a strong radio station in Mexico, and for years raked in a fortune selling his medical miracles. Annoying pressures were brought to bear on him by the medical profession in the U.S., and he was finally forced to shift his headquarters to Del Rio, Mexico. In order to avoid any minor discomforts, John built himself a $200,000 home complete with pool.

Still, the handwriting was on the wall. Throughout the late 1930's the public was becoming more informed, and the governing medical and radio authorities were gaining more control in policing their professions. Despite the tremendous revenue he was generating, the Mexican government forced him to close down the radio station.

The American Medical Association publicly branded him a quack. An indignant John sued them for libel. The jury found the Medical Association innocent, and in fact thought the word quack properly described the particular brand of medicine John was dispensing.

Several men who weren't all that rejuvenated by their goat transplants brought judgments against John. He had to pay damages to satisfy these judgments and little by little he was divested of the trappings of wealth. First the plane went, then the yachts and cars, and finally his home.

In February, 1941 Brinkley declared himself bankrupt. It is estimated that over 200,000 gullible people were bilked out of $10 million by John's various schemes. This figure does not take into account the thousands of nanny goats who became widows due to his machinations.

John never fully recovered from the disgrace of bankruptcy. In May, 1942, at the age of 56, he dropped dead of a heart attack.

THE CAPTAIN OF KOPENICK

The Captain of Kopenick was quite a guy.

Wilhelm Voigt was already in his late 50s in 1906. He had spent many years in jails throughout Germany for petty crimes such as stealing food and clothing. As his record grew longer, his sentences increased correspondingly in length.

Now working long hard hours at his trade, that of a cobbler, the little man with the moustache constantly tried to think of a better way of life. Willie had tried to leave the country, but with his record it was impossible to obtain a passport. In fact, his last two jail sentences had been for trying to steal one from the immigration authorities. Life was one long drag.

Willie lived in East Berlin with his sister and, with each passing day, his moustache grew grayer and his back became more stooped. All around him Prussian pomp and ceremony was being flaunted by strong young men in fancy officer's uniforms. They clicked their heels and snapped salutes, and had the respect of the whole populace.

One day old Willie passed a store window, and from that day on his life was never the same. There, displayed in the window, was a Prussian officer's uniform complete with gold braid. Willie made discreet inquiries. Yes, it was possible. Why not? Then and there Willie decided to transform himself from a weary little shoemaker into a Prussian officer in the Kaiser's army.

He didn't just dash in and purchase the uniform. First there was training to be completed. Willie observed how real officers walked and saluted. He rehearsed before a mirror for hours. He listened to the officers bark out orders to their men. He emulated their actions and their voices. Only when he felt he was absolutely prepared, did he enter the store and purchase the shiny uniform. It didn't quite fit, but it served the purpose.

A little, old cobbler had entered the shop; an officer in the Kaiser's army emerged. Soldiers snapped salutes at Willie. He brought up his right hand in that bored gesture he had worked so hard to perfect. All of a sudden Willie had something which had escaped him all his life—respect.

Willie practised being an officer for many weeks. He had a plan. Returning to his legitimate occupation of cobbler, he travelled a few miles out of Berlin to the town of Kopenick. Willie was particularly interested in the town square and the town hall. He poked around until he was familiar with the location of the various offices.

Willie was ready to put his plan into action. He left his sister's flat as a cobbler carrying a box under his arm. Proceeding directly to the railway station, he locked himself in a restroom. Out popped Wilhelm Voigt, Captain of the Guards.

He then had a short slug of Schnapps at a cafe, and thus fortified, stopped the first five soldiers he met. Actually Willie didn't stop them, he barked, "Halt!" and they damn well snapped to attention. Willie (or maybe we should call him Capt. Voigt) made the Corporal in charge identify himself and the other four men. He then informed them that they were now under his command. While Capt. Voigt was thus engaged another five soldiers happened to be passing. Willie barked his command once again, and so it came to pass that the instant captain had his own private army of 10 men.

Capt. Voigt ordered his men to the railroad station, and the whole kit and kaboodle headed for Kopenick. Capt. Voigt led his men on the march to the town hall.

The good burghers of Kopenick didn't get to see that many military men, and the sight of the elderly captain leading his unit of 10 caused some heads to turn in the small community. Once at the town hall, Capt. Voigt barked out orders. He seemed to know the lay of the land by instinct. The Captain placed guards at all entrances to the building.

Capt. Voigt marched straight into the office of the burgomaster, Dr. Langerhans. Poor Langerhans almost keeled over. Nothing like this had ever happened to him before. Capt. Voigt informed the burgomaster that he was under arrest on the command of His Majesty. When asked for some document or warrant, Capt. Voigt contemptuously informed Langerhans that his soldiers were his warrant.

Once the Captain had this situation well in hand, he proceeded to the office of the Inspector of Police. Voigt explained his mission to the inspector, and at the same time, with his authoritative air, ordered him to attend to the crowd which was now gathering in the town square. The inspector scampered out into the square to keep the peace. Next Capt. Voigt visited the Treasurer's office, confiscated his books and placed him under arrest.

To give you an idea of Voigt's complete command of the situation, the burgomaster actually asked him for permission to meet with his wife. Willie, I mean the Captain, said he could even bring her along, because he was transferring the burgomaster and the treasurer under heavy guard to Berlin. The available cash on hand was to be transferred as well. About 4,000 marks were gathered up, which the Captain nonchalantly placed in a bag. He would take care of the cash personally.

By now rumors had spread throughout the town. Millions of marks had been embezzled by the treasurer and the burgomaster. Hundreds of citizens had gathered to see the fun.

A police officer from the neighboring district of Teltow appeared in front of Capt. Voigt and demanded to know what was going on. Undaunted Capt. Voigt explained the facts to the officer. Taking in the situation at a glance, one of Germany's finest volunteered to assist in any way possible. As a matter of fact, it just so happened that Capt. Voigt needed a man of his calibre to accompany the burgomaster, his wife and the treasurer back to Berlin. He had ordered two closed carriages for this very purpose. A few moments later the carriages arrived and the Teltow officer and his prisoners galloped off to Berlin with instructions from the Captain to report to the proper authorities.

In the meantime Capt. Voigt dismissed his army of 10 men. He hopped the train for Berlin, picked up the box containing his clothing from the checkroom, entered the restroom, and emerged as the cobbler Willie Voigt. Willie hid the money in a deserted shed and went back to his sister's home. The whole operation had taken 12 hours.

The Teltow officer found it difficult to understand why no one was expecting either him or his prisoners. He kept being passed from office to office, until finally he found himself telling his story to the Chief of Police of Berlin and the Adjutant-General, Count Moltke.

The Chief looked at the Adjutant-General and the Adjutant-General looked at the Chief. A light went on. Some little man had duped an entire town. Too many people knew the circumstances to keep it quiet, so it was decided to make the story public and try to apprehend the fugitive. A reward of 2,500 marks was offered for information leading to the capture of the Captain. Even the Kaiser showed an interest and asked to be kept informed of developments.

Despite the German reputation for seriousness, it seems no one could talk or write about the Captain of Kopenick without a chuckle in their hearts and a smile on their lips. Everyone had a good belly laugh. The story spread from Germany throughout the rest of Europe and even to North America.

It took 10 days before the authorities got onto Willie's trail. They traced him through a sabre he had to leave in the restroom. It was too long to fit into the box he had brought for his officer's uniform.

If Willie had caused the world to laugh before, now that he was identified it was even more of a howl. A little jailbird cobbler had been the culprit who had police, soliders, and municipal officials jumping to his command. Willie explained that it really wasn't the money he was after. He had hoped to find a passport in those offices in Kopenick. Besides, it sure was a lot of fun having everyone marching and saluting.

Well, as it turned out, everyone liked Willie. He was a harmless little man. Even during his trial everyone liked him. When the judge sentenced him to four years in jail, he recommended that the accused receive light duties while confined.

In jail everyone sought out Willie's company. He was something of a celebrity. Good behavior earned him his release in 20 months. In August, 1908 he walked out of jail a free man, some say on direct orders of the Kaiser himself.

Such was the affection the German people felt for their self-made instant hero that a committee was formed to provide for Willie. In fact one Berlin family endowed him with 100 marks a month for life. Willie even managed to have quite a show business career. He was in great demand in music halls throughout Europe and appeared on the New York stage. He performed one role only, the one he made famous in real life; that of a German officer shouting out commands. A book was written under his byline entitled "How I Became the Captain of Kopenick". Willie was finally given that which he cherished above all else—a passport. He moved to Luxembourg where he quietly went into retirement.

Willie died in 1922 at the age of 72. He was buried in the cemetary of Our Lady in Luxembourg. When Willie's body was being carried through the gates of the cemetary, as chance would have it, a company of soldiers was marching past. In keeping with a time honored military custom whereby soliders honor the dead, they saluted the hearse. The Captain of Kopenick had received his last salute.

THE GENTLE FORGER

Whenever I think of counterfeiters, I think of well organized gangs who produce and distribute millions of dollars. The greatest counterfeiter the United States has ever known was not a master criminal. No, he was an old man who lived with his dog in a flat on the top floor of a tenement building near Broadway and 96th St. in New York City.

Edward Mueller had for years been a superintendent of apartment buildings until the death of his wife in 1937. With his children grown up and married, he found it difficult at the age of 63 to continue to look after the large buildings. Instead he and his mongrel terrier took a sunny flat of their own, and Mueller decided to become a junk dealer.

He purchased a cart and went about the streets trying to find and buy junk. After a year at this precarious occupation he discovered that he wasn't making enough money to take care of the rather humble needs of himself and his faithful companion. He decided to become a counterfeiter.

Mueller, who was known to all his acquaintances as a sweet tempered, good-natured little guy, went about his task with typical nonchalance. His married daughter happened to have an old studio camera. One day on a visit to her home, he photographed a one dollar bill. Then he made some zinc plates, which he touched up by hand. The finished job looked pretty satisfactory to old Mueller. Later the Secret Service said it was the most amateurish counterfeiting job they had ever come across. In touching up the bogus plates, Mueller had somehow transposed one of the letters in the word WASHINGTON. All his finished bills spelled the word WAHSINGTON. This rather glaring error was never noticed by Mueller or any of his victims.

In November, 1938 Edward Mueller turned out his first

phony bill on his hand driven printing press. He hung the bill up to dry on a clothesline in his flat. The very first bill was used to purchase some junk. Mueller noticed that no one ever took a second look at a one dollar bill.

It was not long before the bills came to the attention of the Secret Service. Not a rash of bills, mind you, more like a trickle. You see, Mueller lacked one quality most counterfeiters have in great abundance. He was not greedy. He printed only enough dollars to take care of the needs of himself and his dog, with one exception. On Sundays he loved to buy enough candy to treat the neighborhood kids.

As the months rolled into years the mysterious counterfeiter who manufactured only ones, and then only in limited quantities, completely baffled the Secret Service. The case had become the longest unsolved counterfeit operation in U.S. history. Who could be turning out 40 or 50 one dollar bills a month and distributing them all over New York City? And such lousy reproductions. Even the paper the money was printed on was of such poor quality that it could be purchased at any corner stationery store. Believe it or not, one of Washington's eyes was an inkblot.

In the first year 585 phony bills were successfully put into circulation. At the end of five years the total had risen to 2,840, or less than two a day. What kind of strange personality was content to turn out such a small quantity of bills. No one seemed to know. Agents swarmed over the area where most of the bills surfaced, but while they uncovered more phony bills all the carriers were victims rather than the culprit they were seeking. From time to time the Secret Service were engaged in other far more important cases, but they always returned to the strange unsolved case of the phony ones.

For 10 years Mueller churned out his incredible product, and was only found out by accident. A fire took place on the top floor of his tenement building. Mueller was not in his flat at the time of the fire, but his pet terrier was suffocated by smoke. The firemen had thrown most of the contents of Mueller's flat into a vacant lot. Mueller went to live with his daughter in the suburbs until his flat could be repaired.

Nine young boys ranging in age from 10 to 15 used the vacant lot as a playground. One of the boys found what he considered to be play money. Adults had been accepting the same quality money as the real thing for 10 years. It seems strange that a 10-year-old immediately recognized it as phony. Another youngster carted home the old printing press. His father saw the boys playing with the money and became suspicious enough to inform the police. One look at the word WAHSINGTON, and the Secret Service knew they were on the trail of their old nemesis. The boys led the police to where they had found the money. It was an easy matter to find out that the press and money had been tossed out of the burned flat.

And who was the tenant of the flat? None other than dear old Edward Mueller. When questioned about his activities, Mueller readily confessed to printing the bills. He explained that in all the years he had been producing the money, he never gave more than one dollar to any one person, and he never made more than he absolutely needed to sustain himself and his dog.

Although Mueller and his phony ones had cost the Secret Service more time and trouble than any other individual counterfeiter, everyone liked the old man. After he was out on bail he became accustomed to dropping in on the authorities to pass the time of day. All five foot three of him would saunter up to the Secret Service offices. To a man, everyone was happy to see him.

When he came to trial, 73-year-old Mueller loved every minute of it. He had been indicted on three counts—possessing plates, passing counterfeit bills, and manufacturing the bills. Mueller was found guilty, and received the light sentence of one year and a day. A fine is mandatory with such a sentence, and a chuckle went through the courtroom when the judge announced the amount of the fine—one dollar.

Edward was released after serving four months, and went to live with his daughter in the suburbs. He loved to relate to friends and neighbors how he had hoodwinked the Secret Service for 10 years. Later a movie was made of Edward's counterfeiting career. Famed character actor Edmund Gwynn played the part of Mueller. Edward attended the movie, and thought it was just great.

THE MONEY MACHINE

Ralph Wilby was born in Weston, Ont. to a hardworking, honest family. After leaving high school, he got a job as a bookkeeper. Ralph put some debits where some credits should have been, and before you could say contingent liability, he was caught and received a year in jail. Released from the inconvenience of this enforced vacation, Ralph next popped up in Norfolk, Va. He sought and obtained gainful employment as a bookkeeper, but it wasn't long before Ralph had his hand in the till again. This time he was deported to Canada.

By this time no legitimate outfit would hire Ralph. It was really too bad because he had decided to turn over a new leaf and go straight. First, though, he had to come up with some scheme to get a job. Leave it to Ralph. He remembered a legitimate accountant named Alexander Douglas Hume, who had worked in both Canada and New York. Mr. Hume had joined the Canadian Army and had been shipped overseas. Ralph decided to take his name. Under the name A. D. Hume, Ralph got a position with the William T. Knopp Management Co. Now in high gear, our hero met Helen Redwin. Helen was the possessor of an hourglass figure and a well turned ankle. Knowing nothing of Ralph's past indiscretions, she became Mrs. A. D. Hume within two weeks.

The happy couple set up housekeeping in a three room apartment in Jackson Heights, a suburb of New York. The Knott Co.'s main function in life was to manage a total of 15 huge department stores. Ralph was by this time a mature 35. He stood 5 ft. 6 ins., had an engaging smile, and was considered a find by the Knott brass. They put Ralph on the audit team checking on the stores. It wasn't long before he gained a reputation for detecting any shortages or outright thefts by employees. Of course we know that Ralph, operating as A. D. Hume, knew the ropes pretty well.

Time passed, and the U.S. entered the war. U.S. citizens were being called into the service, and this caused a hardship to Ralph's company, with many of their top employees being drafted. They took him off the audit team, and with a terrific recommendation from his boss, Mr. Casey, Ralph became assistant auditor stationed at the head office in New York City. While others were being called away to war, Ralph escaped the draft. Canadian military records showed that he was overseas, and American records had him exempt from the draft because he was married. He rose rapidly in the company. He loved his job, his apartment in the suburbs, and his lovely wife Helen.

Then one fine day Mr. Casey took Ralph into a private room and introduced him to an IBM machine. Mr. Casey explained that when manufacturers and wholesalers sold merchandise to any of the 15 Knott department stores, they sent the invoices to this room. The stores checked to see that they received all the merchandise in good order and then they sent along the packing slip. The invoice and packing slip were matched, and then this beautiful IBM machine would spit out the cheque to the supplier. Another machine sitting beside the IBM job signed the cheques with Mr. Casey's signature.

Ralph idly inquired about how many cheques the machine handled. Casey replied that the IBM Machine produced around seven or eight hundred cheques a day, amounting to over $700,000 per week.

Ralph immediately had a frog in his throat. He took out his handkerchief and gently coughed into it.

Mr. Casey put his hand on Ralph's shoulder and told him that from now on he was making him responsible for the cheque-producing IBM machine.

Ralph had an absolute coughing fit.

It was too much for the new leaf that Ralph had turned over. The set-up was ripe for plucking. Ralph decided right then and there to have a go. For starters he sent an invoice to himself from a non-existent firm he called Frederick B. Hecht Co. of St. Louis in the amount of $4,800. Then he sent along the corresponding packing slip, already checked, supposedly from one of the Knott stores. Ralph matched them, gave instructions to his staff, and walked away with a cheque for $4,800. He took a train to St. Louis and showed up at a bank, claiming to be Frederick B. Hecht. He wanted to open an account and was greeted with open arms. There was one thing though; he really should have some sort of references. No problem. Ralph told the manager to dash off a letter to the William T. Knott Co. of New York, Attention Mr. A. D. Hume, and he should receive a reference by return mail. Ralph left the 48 bills for deposit as soon as the manager received the reference letter.

Ralph scampered back to New York and waited for the bank manager's letter to himself. Sure enough, it arrived and Ralph answered that the Frederick B. Hecht firm was above reproach. The manager was delighted to deposit the cheque.

To balance the books, Ralph made up minute charges and spread the $4,800 over the 15 stores. It was peanuts to an outfit doing $40 million a year. Ralph repeated this basic scheme over and over until he had deposits in every city close to New York. The take amounted to over $100,000.

Was Ralph happy? Well, no, he wasn't. For one thing, he was doing extremely well at his legitimate occupation, and liked his job and his pretty wife in the suburbs. For another thing, he was working like a dog, making trips out of town depositing cheques' and the paperwork involved was getting too much for him. He started to look peaked. All in all, Ralph figured it wasn't worth it and he decided to give back all the money. He thought and thought, but it was no use. That IBM machine giveth but it just wasn't equipped to taketh away: Ralph couldn't give back the money without exposing himself.

Then the little con man had another turn of mind. Why be small potatoes? Ralph accelerated his fraud, and within three months had deposits of over $400,000. Then, out of the blue, a man named Davidson who worked for an organization called the F.B.I. called on Ralph. He wanted to know if he knew a Frederick B. Hecht. Ralph almost passed out. He had made up the name. What could the F.B.I. want with Hecht? Ralph figured the feds were onto his scheme and were playing cat and mouse with him. He was wrong. All they were inquiring about was a routine check of German sounding names, who had recently changed domiciles. One way to accomplish this was by checking bank accounts that suddenly were transferred or closed.

Ralph put Davidson off for a week, and withdrew cash from all his accounts. He ended up with $400,000 in a cardboard box. Then he told Mr. Casey he was taking his long overdue vacation. Ralph and the wife left that very day, and didn't stop until they hit Victoria, B.C.

Ralph never did return from his vacation. Davidson of the F.B.I. contacted Mr. Casey and told him of trying to trace a Mr. Hecht through Ralph.

Whenever a fellow disappears who has control over an IBM cheque writing machine, his superiors tend to have headaches. Mr. Casey had a throbbing migraine.

It took a lot of digging, but they finally uncovered Ralph's fictitious companies. The authorities then went into Mr. A. D. Hume's background and found he was really overseas with the Canadian Army. They ended up with our friend Ralph Wilby of Weston and his rather illuminating police record.

Well, the ledgers hit the fan. Police started tracing Ralph and Helen, finally catching up with them in the nice little house they had bought in Victoria. He had left New York as A. D. Hume, and was brought back as Ralph Wilby, con artist extraordinaire. He was of particular interest to an insurance company that stood to lose a bundle unless he came up with the $400,000. Finally he made a deal. Ralph figured he had spent $10,000 of his own money on expenses travelling around the country perpetrating his con. He said he would give back everything he had left if they gave him $10,000 for his trouble. The insurance company jumped at the proposition. Ralph directed the R.C.M.P. to some tin cans he had buried in his back yard in Victoria, where almost all the money was recovered.

Ralph got seven years in Sing Sing. Helen, who never knew a thing about Ralph's illegal activities, got a divorce. Ralph served his seven years in Sing Sing, and upon his release received his $10,000 and was deported back to Canada.

I don't know where Ralph Wilby is now. Perhaps that unobtrusive little guy in your accounts payable department . . . nah, it couldn't be!

ELIJAH THE RESTORER

It is hard to say just when John Alexander Dowie, better known as Elijah the Restorer, decided that money and sex were the most important things in life. It is even more difficult to pinpoint the exact moment when the Restorer decided to embrace religion.

John Dowie was born in 1847 in Edinburgh, Scotland. When he was 13 his family emigrated to Australia. John took to reading the Bible. He worked hard, saved his pennies, and returned to Scotland to study for the ministry. Four years later he came back to Australia where, at the age of 25, he was ordained a Congressionalist Minister. John settled down for a while, but soon tired of the ministry, and became an evangelist taking the good word to the Australian countryside.

Along the way John, who had the same normal urges as the rest of us mortals, met a rather angelic young lady with the unbelievable name of Jane Wrath. It wasn't long before Jane became Mrs. Dowie. Despite suffering from annoying headaches, she joined her husband in spreading the gospel.

One day, quite by accident, John mentioned to a group of the faithful who had gathered to be saved, that he had laid hands upon Jane's headache wracked head, and lo and behold, her headaches disappeared, vanished, caput, never to return. John was as surprised as anyone to find out that from this humble beginning people started to come to him to be healed. They even gave him freewill offerings for the promise of a cure.

John, not one to look a heavenly gift horse in the mouth, quickly formed the Divine Healing Association to handle the flow of hard cash. For six years he healed, and the suckers paid. Still, he thought, bigger and better things must lie in store for him in America. In 1888, with the faithful Jane by his side, he set sail for San Francisco, ostensibly to form another branch of his association. He wandered across the land, setting up several branch healing offices, but when he set foot in Chicago he knew he had really arrived. If ever a place needed saving and healing, it was Chicago.

John eyed the Chicago World's Fair being held in 1893 with the anticipation of a carny operator. He set up his tabernacle close by the main gates of the fair, and started preaching and healing. Business was so good he was at it 15 hours a day, seven days a week. He even managed to collect enough crutches and canes to form a respectable backdrop for his preaching platform. Money was pouring in from his branch offices. By 1895 he had become a money making machine and a confirmed enemy of legitimate doctors. While the established medical authorities agreed that emotion and psychology played some part in therapy, they claimed that John was causing all kinds of human misery by keeping his followers from seeking medical attention. Our hero fought the establishment at every opportunity, and kept on counting the cash.

John bought a seven story building on Michigan Ave. He and Jane occupied two luxurious floors. Each Sunday he preached to a packed audience in the Chicago auditorium. He was making so much money he formed his own bank, the Zion City Bank, to look after his investments. Quietly John, who had a definite flair for finance, picked up 6,500 acres between Chicago and Milwaukee. To put together the huge package John had shelled out $1,250,000.

Dowie then announced that he was forming the Christian Catholic Church in Zion, and that all his faith healing branches were henceforth to direct their incomes to this new religion. Once this little transaction was successfully completed, John took off for Europe to set up still more faith healing operations.

When he returned, he had another blockbuster to unload on the public. He intended to form his own city on the land which he controlled. It was to be called Zion. John stated that he was the reincarnation of the prophet Elijah, and those who followed him to his new city would, of course, have to consider him their new God. Not everyone accepted this garbage at face value. Legitimate religious organizations ridiculed Elijah the Restorer, as he was called, but enough of the faithful followed blindly to make the scheme a success.

Five thousand souls started to build the city of Zion for their leader and themselves. Factories, a bank, and a college were all constructed and all, of course, belonged to Elijah. It is estimated that by 1901 John's little personal empire had assets worth over $5 million. There was no stopping our boy. He built a bakery and factories producing soap and candy. He alone appointed the mayor and all the officials of Zion. He even had his own army. Elijah called them the Zion Guard, and outfitted them in outlandish uniforms embroidered with doves of peace.

At age 55, and at the height of his career, Elijah took to spending more and more time at his summer home. On a warm summer evening he could be seen entering the luxurious $200,000 home away from home with a female member of his flock. It appears that Elijah still had those desires he always had as plain John Dowie.

Elijah made a fatal mistake. Now worth an estimated $23 million, he decided to tackle New York City. He sent thousands of advance men to set up accommodations for a crusade he planned for the month of October, 1903. He rented Madison Square Garden, and poured hundreds of thousands of dollars into the publicity campaign for his crusade.

Complete with choir and long flowing gowns, Elijah opened his crusade before a packed Madison Square Gardens audience of 12,000. Elijah had miscalculated the gullibility of his big city audience. As he tore into the sins of urban life, the crowd who had heard the same thing many times before, started to boo the great one. Thousands got up and left. The second night his audience had dwindled to 6,000. Each successive night was worse. The debacle had cost Elijah a fortune.

Worse still, because of the many months of massive effort which had gone into saving souls in New York, his own City of Zion had started to go under from neglect. Not wanting to face reality, Elijah took off for Mexico to open still more healing establishments. When he returned, it was too late. Zion was having trouble paying its bills. In the end the courts declared the city bankrupt and placed its affairs in the hands of a receiver.

It never rains but it pours. Some indiscreet lady picked this inopportune moment to tell all about Elijah's little capers in the summer house. It didn't help matters that she was a married woman. Soon other married ladies came forward and spilled the beans about Elijah and his dalliances.

Elijah's wife Jane announced that she was leaving the great one. This was the last straw. Depressed and heartbroken at his sudden and swift downfall, Elijah went to bed one evening in March, 1907 and died in his sleep.

Unbelievably, a disciple of Elijah's, one Wilbur Voliva, started to raise money by preaching much the same line as his predecessor. Little by little he succeeded in raising enough money to satisfy creditors, until in the end he was able to bring Zion out of hock. He died in 1942.

Today, some of the children of the followers of Elijah and Voliva, still live in Zion. Without a doubt it is a town with one of the strangest histories in America, founded by one of the greatest con artists the world has ever known.

THE DIAMOND MANUFACTURER

It is one thing to con an old lady out of a few thousand dollars, and quite another to tackle one of the most powerful companies in the world and take them to the cleaners.

Henri Lemoine did.

Henri was born in Paris to a very prominent family. He excelled in school and was getting straight A's in college right up until the time he sold the dormitory to his classmates. This necessitated a hasty exit and spelled the end of Henri's formal education. Various activities followed. Henri talked some fool into believing he was the heir of Louis XIV. It cost the poor sucker 1,000 pounds to be called king for a few days. Of course, in the off season Henri sold the Eiffel Tower to gullible Americans. Occasionally Henri was caught while perpetrating his cute little capers, which would result in his being hauled off to prison. Each time he was released he pulled a bigger and better con. Through it all Henri was married to a real doll who knew that hubby operated outside the law. Like Henri, she liked the money and loved the thrill of it all.

In January, 1905 Lemoine, hat in hand, called at the office of Henry Feldenheimer, one of Paris' most prominent diamond dealers. Henri reached across a desk and passed over six uncut diamonds to Feldenheimer. Adjusting his jeweller's glass, Feldenheimer said, "Remarkable. Absolutely remarkable. They're absolutely perfect."

You see, there was nothing remarkable about the stones themselves, just the fact that Henri claimed to have manufactured them by artificial means. Naturally, Henri was in that office to obtain financial assistance because his experiments had supposedly wiped him out. Now that he was ready to start production, he needed further cash for new facilities.

Feldenheimer said he needed a few days. Taking the stones, he set up a meeting with Sir Julius Werhner, one of the governors of De Beers Consolidated Mines Ltd., the great South African diamond company. The thought of artifical diamonds had almost the same effect on Sir Julius as the advent of the automobile must have had on horseshoe manufacturers. Sir Julius developed a little twitch in the corner of his mouth.

Not being a gullible man, Sir Julius wanted to see Henri actually produce diamonds. Feldenheimer said this could be arranged, but first he had to attend to a little detail. The detail was a quick legal document drawn up between himself and our Henri, giving Feldenheimer 10 per cent of anything that would ever be realized from the invention of artifical diamonds.

And so it came to pass on a dark starless night in Paris there was a meeting in an attic apartment. In attendance were Feldenheimer, Sir Julius, Francis Oaks, a director of De Beers; and Alfred Beit, a financier.

Henri shouted from behind a curtain for his distinguished guests to be seated. Once they were comfortable, the curtains parted and there stood Henri in front of his extensively equipped laboratory. With a backdrop of bubbling vessels, retorts, and test tubes, Henri faced some of the most powerful men in the world completely nude, wearing only shoes and socks. His eyes twinkled as he explained to his startled audience that he wanted to make it perfectly clear that he had nothing hidden on his person.

The focal point of Lemoine's lab was a small furnace. He explained that by heating carbon and his secret ingredient, and sending an electric current through the mass, he could produce diamonds. To demonstrate he held a round pottery jar filled with carbon and his supposedly secret substance.

All the sceptics examined the jar and, convinced that there were no diamonds hidden in the dark substance, they returned the jar to Henri, who placed it in the furnace. An hour later Henri, still naked as the day he was born, pulled the jar out of the furnace and out popped 25 rough diamonds. The astonished audience asked for an instant replay. An hour later Henri produced another 30 diamonds.

Sir Julius offered Henri the equivalent of $50,000 right there and then for his secret formula. Henri, cool customer that he was, said he wanted it in writing so he could think it over. Then he made a counter offer. He would write out the formula with the stipulation that it not be revealed to anyone until after his death. In the meantime he would stop making diamonds. Sir Julius went for it. A sealed envelope went into the safety deposit box, Henri got the 50 big ones, and the De Beers group figured they had saved their organization from financial ruin by keeping cheap diamonds from being dumped on the market.

Then Henri Lemoine went for broke. He suggested to the De Beers boys that they should manufacture diamonds for industrial purposes. Feldenheimer, who was getting 10 per cent of all the action, pushed the scheme with Sir Julius. Believe it or not, the De Beers group went to the well again. This time they fell hook, line and sinker. They appointed Henri to build a turbo electric plant in Angeliers to produce the industrial diamonds. They wired him a quick $100,000 for starters from Africa. Several months later Henri hired a photographer to take a picture of a real turbo electric plant. He sent it to his backers in Africa. They were so delighted with the progress they hurried off another $100,000. Incredible as it sounds, Henri kept sucking money out of his African partners for three years. Each time he appeared close to production, another unfortunate delay took place, requiring more money. Finally the fish down in the Dark Continent decided to take a little swim to France to see the plant. They found a muncipal plant just like the pictures they had received over the years. The police were consulted, and of course Henri's past was revealed to his erstwhile associates. They also found that not only had Henri built a nonexistent plant, he was also an expert at slight of hand. The police suggested that Henri had probably palmed the diamonds, and slipped them into the container just before he placed the jar into the furnace.

Henri was picked up and placed in jail. Not exactly a dummy, Henri got a lawyer. His lawyer maintained that Henri did nothing wrong. He said that Henri's wife took all the African money, divorced Henri, and disappeared. His client had been forced to deceive his partners. They had shown up too soon. For another paltry $90,000 Henri would produce the diamonds under supervision.

Truth is stranger than fiction. Sir Julius advanced Henri

another $90,000. Henri started construction, then the delays started again. Patience ran out and so did Henri. He skipped the night before the authorities were going to pick him up. A short time later he was spotted on the streets of Paris. He was arrested, and spent six years in prison. They opened the safety deposit box, and Henri's note read, "It is very difficult to make diamonds."

Don't shed too many tears for our hero. From that January day in 1905, when he walked into Feldenheimer's office and professed to be able to make diamonds, he had taken the De Beers organization for an estimated half million dollars.

No one recovered a penny.

Once released from prison, he completely disappeared, and has never been heard of since.

However, there are those who knew Henri who swear they have seen him since his release in the company of his wife.

No, it couldn't be—not after the divorce, not the six years in prison; or could this have been Henri's biggest con of all.

THE SPANISH CONNECTION

You might wonder why some gentlemen become small time con artists instead of big time con artists. The answer is obvious. You don't require that much brain power to become a small change arist. Ah, but to become a con artist where the stakes are counted in the millions of dollars is quite another ball of wax.

Take Don James Addison de Peralta-Reavis, for example. Don appeared on the scene in 1883 in Arizona. All he claimed to be was the owner of the entire state. He said that he came to claim his inheritance, Le Baronia de Arizonae, which was granted by King Ferdinand of Spain to a Don Miguel on Dec. 20, 1748. Naturally our Don was the living descendant of Don Miguel and the rightful owner of most of the counties of Arizona, as well as the city of Phoenix.

At first Don was met with a certain amount of ridicule. The enormity of his claim was beyond belief. Of course, if by any remote possibility it was valid, then everyone who owned a lot of land within the Baronia was susceptible to being dispossessed. Not only that, but all the mines, property, and anything of value would revert into the hand of Don James Addison de Peralta-Reavis, as Don liked to be called.

He hired a battery of top notch lawyers to assert his claim. With Don acting as his own publicity agent, he went about holding public meetings, explaining how the whole thing happened.

Don was a real charmer. He stated that he had no intention of being cruel or cheating anyone. It just so happened that Arizona, which had at one time been a part of Mexico, had been granted to an antecedent of his. Don had all the legal documentation necessary to back his claim. In fact, he was darn fair about the whole thing. He only wanted a small rent from everyone living on his land. Of course, the large producing silver mines would be taxed at a somewhat more ambitious rate.

The state of Arizona formed a committee to investigate Don's claim. This thing was becoming serious. All the maps and documents were examined, and the committee became convinced that they were genuine. The legalities were checked in Washington, and eventually an emissary was sent to Spain. Old records were checked and rechecked. There seemed to no doubt about it; everything appeared to be exactly as Don had said all along. The king of Spain had indeed granted the area that was presently Arizona to the heirs of Don Miguel. The committee in its wisdom did bring up the fact that our Don had to prove that he was a descendant of Don Miguel, and that he was the only living descendant.

Don didn't blink an eye. He brought forth genealogical tables showing that only two descendants of Don Miguel were alive. One of course was himself. The other was a female descendant, Sofia Loreta Micaela. Then Don really pulled the carpet out from under the committee. He introduced them to his wife, none other than Sofia Loreta Micaela de Peralta-Reavis.

It took almost a year to trace and verify the claims of the Baron and Baroness, but in the end their claim was accepted as legitimate. Thousands of hardworking homesteaders paid a small amount each month to their new landlords. More substantial concerns, like the Southern Pacific Railway, anted up $50,000 for the right to move their trains through Don's property. In a short time our hero became a multimillionaire, and one of the most influential men in the western United States. Don lived like a king. He had what amounted to palaces in St. Louis, Washington, Madrid and Mexico City.

Unbelievably, Don ruled over his domain for 10 long years. Now and then some agency or committee would be formed to try to find some fraudulent act or phony document in the Baron's string of documents. All attempts to discredit our hero failed. Then one day a private detective, working secretly for private concerned individuals, was poring over documents in the archives of Spain. While holding one of the documents dated 1759 up to the light, the detective noticed the watermark of a paper producing mill in Wisconsin. There surely was no one producing paper in Wisconsin in 1759.

A long series of revelations followed, whereby Don was proved to be a fake. Jimmy Reavis was really born in Missouri. He had discovered that he had an uncanny ability to copy signatures. While in the Confederate Army he had made quite a name for himself by selling his particular service to forge weekend passes for his buddies.

After the war he worked as a streetcar conductor in St. Louis, and then gravitated to real estate. It wasn't long before he obtained a job in the land office of the U.S. government. Because of treaties with Mexico, he found that part of his job was studying the validity of land claims. In this way he became knowledgeable about what constitutes a legitimate land claim.

His scheme took over two years in preparation. He studied the Spanish language and even acquired Spanish mannerisms. Then he travelled to Mexico City, Washington, and Madrid, where he spent days in the old churches and archives. Painstakingly he gradually substituted forged documents for the genuine articles.

Don found a servant girl he could trust. He groomed and molded her as his wife and partner. When the true facts about Don were revealed, he and his wife disappeared and never surfaced again.

If you want to discount the $28 the Indians were paid for Manhattan, Don had pulled off the largest and most successful land swindle in the history of American real estate.

A BETTER IDEA

David Morton Roll had the appearance of a prosperous, high level executive. He dressed immaculately in expensive tailor-made pinstripe suits, which were enhanced by solid gold tie clips and cufflinks. His lean body and honest face oozed confidence. As well they might—you see, Dave was one of the coolest confidence men who ever lived.

Like many a small time practitioner of the con, Dave lived for the big score. That's how he came to be chauffeur-driven in an over-sized limousine to the elegant Shoreham Hotel in Washington, D.C. When Dave checked in, he let it be known that he was in somewhat of a rush. An important appointment with the Secretary of the Interior, no less. He'd be back for dinner, and would the clerk kindly let him know when Henry Ford's telephone call came through.

Well, now, that's a pretty fair country entrance in anyone's book. In the Washington of 1931 it stamped David Morton Roll as a man of influence. The slick con man wasn't through yet. Not by a long shot.

Sure enough, during dinner a telephone call came through from Henry Ford for Dave Roll. The pageboy shouted the names loud and clear throughout the lobby. When Dave took the call on the lobby phone he talked loudly enough so that he almost registered on a seismograph in Hoboken. He let drop key words like Muscle Shoals and $88 million. That was enough.

In 1931 Muscle Shoals was a 38 mile strip of the Tennessee River where the water fell in a steep grade for 135 feet. The rapids had tremendous water power potential. The U.S. Department of the Interior was considering developing it or privately leasing out the area for 99 years. The well-informed in Washington knew that Henry Ford had already tried un-

135

successfully to purchase Muscle Shoals on two different occasions. Dave Roll knew too.

The sting was in. The news spread like wildfire. Henry
Ford's top advisor was in town with 88 big ones to purchase
Muscle Shoals. Soon invitations arrived at the Shoreham.
Dave was being invited on the party circuit as he knew he
would. Outfitted with white tails, the 42-year-old con man
made a dashing figure at Washington's elegant watering
holes. One thing, though, Dave wouldn't accept a cigarette
nor, heaven forbid, take a drink. Everyone knew that back
home in Dearborn, Henry didn't approve of such vulgar
habits.

Dave made a terrific impression. At one of these forays he
met Robert Latham Owen, who had served as senator from
Oklahoma for 18 years. Owen, who knew everyone who was
anyone, had stayed on in Washington to practise law. He
heard that Roll was in Washington to negotiate the purchase
of Muscle Shoals for Henry Ford. The senator came right
out and asked Dave if he could be his legal representative
for the upcoming deal. Cunning Dave said he would be
considered.

The very next day Owen visited Roll at the Shoreham.
Things started to pop. Dave received two phone calls, supposedly from Henry Ford himself. Then he revealed the
details of his association with the automobile magnate. He
showed the now drooling Owen documents purportedly from
Ford, stating that Ford was willing to pay 88 million dollars
for Muscle Shoals. If Dave paid anything less than 88 million, he was to keep the difference. Should the deal not go
through, Dave was to be paid a flat fee of $250,000 for his
services.

Owen was gasping for air. The hook was well planted. If
the deal went through for say 80 mil, Roll stood to make a
cool $8 million. The legal fees would be worth a fortune to
the firm picked to guide the deal through the government
and the courts.

Dave looked Owen in the eye and said, "You are our legal
representative on the Muscle Shoals project. The fee is
$100,000 per year." It would, however, be necessary for
Owen to accompany Dave to Dearborn, Mich., to meet Mr.
Ford. Dear Henry insisted on meeting his senior people.

Owen, smelling cash, would have hitchhiked to Dearborn that same night.

Within a few days Dave and Owen checked into the Book-Cadillac Hotel in Detroit. On the first morning, while Dave was out for a walk, the phone rang. The caller identified himself as Henry Ford. Once Ford found out that Dave wasn't in he spoke to Owen. He said he was embarrassed as he would not be able to meet with the two men. He had to leave town immediately on other business. Would Senator Owen mind answering a few questions on the phone. You bet your bottom dollar the senator didn't mind. Well, old Henry took the senator over the coals for about 20 minutes, covering every aspect of Owen's life. He ended the conversation by telling Owen to have Dave draw up an employment contract. The senator was Henry's kind of man.

Owen was ecstatic at the pleasant turn of events. Dave seemed less than pleased. On the return train trip to Washington, Owen inquired as to what was wrong. Dave reluctantly revealed that despite apparently wallowing in money, ready cash was a problem. He told Owen that he had just made a $2 million settlement on his wife in order to obtain a divorce. The divorce had not been amicable, and had resulted in legal fees of $200,000. Dave found himself short a paltry $57,000.

"Not to worry, Dave, my boy, let me advance you the fifty seven thou." It was to be the first of many annoying little sums that the senator was to pass on to Dave Roll.

Just as Senator Owen had been lured into the trap, scores of other lawyers tried to approach Dave. They found out it wasn't easy. Out of the woodwork emerged one J. Jones. Jones acted as a buffer. He let it be known that if you wanted to do business with Dave Roll, you had to go through J. Jones. The Jones boy also let it be known that his boss always took his recommendations. May the saints preserve us, J. Jones also let it be known that he was on the take. He could obtain legal work amounting to hundreds of thousands of dollars for little gratuities of $5,000 here and $10,000 there. Complete secrecy was to be maintained until the deal was official. Oh, yes, cash in advance, if you please.

It is estimated that Dave and Jones, whoever he was, picked up $150,000 on this little sideline. Later, many of the lawyers taken by this scheme didn't come forward. They were none too anxious to let it be known that they had offered bribes.

It is a tribute to David Roll's gall that he lived in the lap of luxury for approximately three years while fleecing Senator Owen. Owen never received one cent, but as Roll later said, he didn't do a scrap of work, either.

The Senator became concerned when Dave's loans reached $200,000. To alleviate his fears, Dave signed a document guaranteeing one half of his anticipated total income from the Muscle Shoals deal. Owen figured that he had just cut himself in for approximately $4 million.

Dave kept the sham going as long as he could. Roosevelt defeated Hoover, helping him stall a while longer. In one fell swoop, the cat came jumping out of the bag. Roosevelt announced that the government was creating the Tennessee Valley Authority, which encompassed the Muscle Shoals development.

Owen was beside himself. He dashed off to Detroit, and this time actually met with Henry Ford. His worst fears became reality. Henry Ford had never heard of Dave Roll. Owen practically ran back to Washington. This time he had a friendly little chat with J. Edgar Hoover of the F.B.I. Lo and behold, J. Edgar found out that Dave Roll had previously been detained as an unpaid guest at the Colorado State Penetentiary for five years. Upon his release Dave had rushed directly from the penal institution into Senator Owen's open arms in Washington.

How did he do it? Roll's suckers were not dummies. They were senators, lawyers, and even judges. Yet the ex con was able to fool them all. He had so much gall he had never even changed his name. It does well to understand that when you are dealing in millions, $50,000 is not a great deal of money. When you are dealing in contracts amounting to hundreds of thousands of dollars, $5,000 is not a large amount. Roll was astute enough to realize this. Like all other con men, he played on one human frailty—greed.

Dave was picked up while having a steak in the Shoreham's dining room. He was charged with obtaining money under false pretenses. While in jail awaiting trial, Dave lived high off the hog. He had food, booze, and women delivered to the jail. He became one of the most popular prisoners ever held in Washington.

On June 12, 1934, his bail was reduced to $7,500. Dave handed over the cash and left Washington. To pass the time while awaiting trial, he took a luxury suite at the Ritz Carlton Hotel in Atlantic City. For almost a month the champagne flowed.

On July 4, Dave doubled over in pain. Rushed to the hospital, he died on the operating table. Everyone knew David Morton Roll had more than an adequate supply of gall, but no one knew he had gallstones.

ANYBODY WANT TO BUY THE EIFFEL TOWER?

The mayor of Hostinne was a happy man that day in 1890 when his son Victor popped into the world. The affairs of the small town situated along the River Elbe in a section of Czechoslovakia known as Bohemia came to an abrupt stop. Little Victor Lustig would have the best education that money could buy. He would attend a private school in Dresden, then on to university, then who knows—a renowned scientist, perhaps an eminent doctor. If Poppa only knew. Would you believe one of the most innovative and slippery confidence men the world has ever known?

The first part of the mayor's dream for his son came true. In his formative years Victor was shipped off to a boarding school in Dresden. After graduation he thought he would try his luck in Paris. Naturally he told his ever-trusting father that he was attending the Sorbonne, thereby assuring himself of a monthly stipend to keep body and soul together.

Now a tall, slim debonaire young man, he taught himself the intricacies of poker until there were few who had a chance sitting at the same table with him. He called himself Count Lustig, and plied his trade on the luxury liners crossing the Atlantic. One of Victor's colleagues on the ocean liners was the well known American gambler, Nicky Arnstein. The two became great friends and often combined their talents to fleece the wealthy industrialists. To alleviate the tedium of the ocean voyage Victor wasn't adverse to bedding down with a businessman's wife when the occasion presented itself.

In 1914 the war came along, effectively putting an end to his Atlantic gambling days, but bigger and better things were in store for the Count.

Equipped with $25,000 in profits from his gambling operations, Count Lustig found a plum just waiting to be plucked. One day during the war an unwary banker named Green in a small Kansas town was visited by a slim European, obviously a man of substance. Count Lustig had cased his mark well in advance. He knew the banker had a derelict, almost worthless, farm which he was itching to unload. The Count explained to banker Green that he had been forced to leave his native Austria, and he was looking for a place to retire on a piece of land which he could turn into an estate. Green's eyes lit up like lanterns. He showed Lustig the farm that same day.

Back in the bank office Lustig took out $50,000 in bonds and offered $25,000 in cash for the farm. Had Green been an honest man he would have told the Count that the farm was only worth $5,000, but he chose to keep quiet. The Count had figured his sucker's reaction perfectly. A deal was struck. Green offered to cash the bonds. Count Lustig would sign off the bonds and would receive the deed to the farm and his change of $25,000 in cash in return for the bonds that evening.

The two men sipped a Cointreau while they completed the deal. The Count walked off with the $25,000 in cash and Green received a neatly wrapped parcel of bonds. A few hours later Green opened up his packet of bonds only to find cut up newspapers. A badly perspiring banker frantically knocked on the Count's hotel room door. The Count was long gone.

Count Lustig travelled the world living in the lap of luxury. He wore the best clothing, dined in the best restaurants and courted the most attractive women. He worked hard at his trade.

Take the time he sold the Eiffel Tower for example. In 1925 there was a lot of publicity given to the fact that the Eiffel Tower required a great deal of money to keep it in proper repair. Some were in favor of tearing it down altogether, and it was this news which gave the Count his great idea.

Staying at the plush Hotel Crillon, the Count had some impressive, but phony, letterheads printed. On this stationery purportedly from the Deputy Director-General of the Ministere des Postes et Telegraphes, he invited Paris' leading scrap dealers to a meeting to discuss a government contract.

Posing as a senior government official he explained to the gathering, in confidence, that the Eiffel Tower was to be dismantled and the 7,000 tons of scrap iron was to be sold. Those present were the select few being invited to tender. The highest bidder would, of course, receive the contract.

All during the meeting the Count was studying the businessmen looking for his mark. He found him in the person of Monsieur Andre Poisson, a man a bit less cultured than his companions—a man looking for an edge.

That same night the Count called Monsieur Poisson to his suite. He explained that government officials didn't make a great deal of money. Poisson didn't need any more of a hint. He produced a wad of bills. With a twinkle in his eye, the Count pocketed the cash. He presented Poisson with an impressive looking contract, and a promise that he would inform the unsuccessful competitors in the morning.

The next day the Count had left France and was luxuriating with a lady friend in Germany. The caper never did get much publicity. M. Poisson thought that discretion was the better part of valor. He kept his mouth shut.

The Eiffel Tower scam was so successful that two years later the Count dug up some more scrap dealers and sold the Tower for the second time. This time the victim screamed, so the Count had to retire from the Tower selling business.

All his life Victor came up with novel schemes to part the greedy from their money. Once he even borrowed $50,000 from the notorious Al Capone with a promise that he would double the money for the gangster in 60 days. When he showed up with the $50,000 and explained that his scheme had failed, old Scarface was so impressed that he gave Lustig $5,000 as a reward for being so honest. That old twinkle came to the Count's eye. He again had exactly figured out his score's reaction.

All things come to an end. The Count entered the unfamiliar field of counterfeiting, working as a distributor, and was caught by the F.B.I. In 1936 he was sentenced to 20 years in Alcatraz. The man who sold the Eiffel Tower twice, died in prison.

One wonders if he ever ran across his old pal Capone in Alcatraz. At the time, Al had a job there in the laundry.

STANLEY RULED THE WAVES

What makes some men want to be somebody else? Usually the answer is money or power. It's not often that an imposter arrives upon the scene with no thought of hard cash hidden in the far recesses of his mind.

Stanley Clifford Weyman was one of those men who loved being an imposter for only the action and fun. He had a sense of the ridiculous that has rarely been duplicated.

Born in 1890 in Brooklyn, New York, to poor immigrant parents, Stanley longed for an education. Because his parents could ill afford to send him to school, he was forced to go to work at an early age. The young boy grew up to be a shy little man. Stanley always envied those lucky people in our society who were able to command respect, those action people who made the world go around.

There was one way to become important, and Stanley took that one way. He would pretend. Stanley Weyman worked at some menial task for a year or two, but always he would leave his job suddenly and assume a role, not for money, but for the hell of it.

One fine day, while the First World War was being fought in the trenches of Europe, Stanley decided to become a Lieutenant Commander in, of all things, the Rumanian Army. While he was at it he became the Rumanian Consul General in New York City. Stanley got the notion that he wanted to inspect a battleship.

With about as much thought as you would give to crossing the street, Stanley called the U.S. Navy Department in Washington. After the usual amenities, he mentioned that the Queen of Rumania had assigned him the pleasant task of bringing greetings from his country to the U.S. The Queen had mentioned that the inspection of warship might be a nice gesture.

That's how Stanley Weyman, the Brooklyn store clerk, was given every courtesy of the U.S. Navy as he was piped aboard the U.S.S. Wyoming. Stan looked just great in his powder blue uniform trimmed in gold. At the age of 24 he had managed to hoodwink the entire U.S. Navy. After the inspection he rented a private dining room at the Astor Hotel, and had all the brass over for a sumptuous meal. The tab? Don't bother me with such details. Send it along to the Rumanian Consulate in Washington.

Later, the party was over in more ways than one for the bogus Rumanian. Stan was traced and apprehended. He cheerfully spent two years in jail.

In 1920 Stanley read an ad in the newspaper that seemed tailor made for him. A New York development company was looking for a doctor to travel to Lima, Peru, to inspect sanitation conditions in that city. It was duck soup for our boy to lay his hands on phony credentials. With a name change here and a name change there, Stanley became Dr. S. Weyman. He so impressed the legitimate doctor reviewing the applicants that he got the job. Dr. Weyman arrived in Lima and did what he usually did. He threw a party.

Everyone liked the doctor, and the doctor liked parties, servants, and new cars. In the sanitation department Stan went along with anything which looked like a good suggestion. It was the best he could do. He had no idea what anyone was talking about.

Back home his company couldn't believe the fantastic expense accounts. They were just too much. Who was this Dr. Weyman anyway? A closer scrutiny of his credentials revealed his true identity. Quietly and without fuss, Dr. Weyman was brought home and relieved of his duty. Gee, it had been great fun.

Stanley had hardly shaken the dust of Peru off his boots when he noticed another startling announcement in the newspapers. Princess Fatima of Afghanistan was not receiving the usual welcome afforded royalty while visiting the U.S. Stanley decided to change all that. Before you could say Charlie Chaplin, a dapper little man in top hat and cane presented himself to the Princess at her hotel. Under Secretary Stanley

Clifford Weyman of the U.S. State Department at your service. Fatima was delighted.

Stanley explained that his mission was to escort the Princess to Washington, where she was to meet the Secretary of State and the President. First, of course, it was quite normal for the Princess to place $10,000 in his hands so that he could purchase gifts for the personnel at the State Department and the White House, as was the custom. Fatima slipped Stan the ten big ones.

Stanley didn't have honest-to-goodness larceny in his heart. He used the money wisely. First he hired a private railway car for the Royal entourage. Upon arrival in Washington, he ensconced the whole kit and kaboodle in the Willard Hotel. Stan looked sharp in his Lieutenant Commander's whites as he advised the State Department that he was assigned to arrange a meeting between Princess Fatima and the Secretary of State, Charles Evans Hughes.

A reception was duly arranged, and Fatima and Hughes got along just swell. Toward the end of the evening Lt. Comm. Weyman told Hughes that it was the Princess' fond wish to meet the President of the U.S. Hughes went to a phone. It was all fixed. Weyman, Fatima, Hughes, and a few bodyguards crossed the street to the White House. The clerk from Brooklyn spent a pleasant half hour swapping yarns with Warren G. Harding, the President of the United States.

The Navy brass did a routine check on Weyman that came up ex con. The very next day they swooped down on Weyman's hotel suite. The little commander was long gone. When the story broke in the newspapers, a wide smile crossed the face of a shy clerk in Brooklyn.

When Rudolph Valentino died in 1926, Pola Negri appeared in New York. She locked herself in a suite in the Ambassador Hotel, supposedly heartbroken over the great lover's death. The word out of her hotel was that she had taken ill because of her great loss. Medical bulletins issued from her suite came from none other than Dr. Stanley Weyman. It was simple. Stan merely showed up at the hotel one day and told Pola that he had been Rudy's doctor. He knew that Rudy would want him to look after her. Stan moved right into the suite.

Later, the little imposter, who always used his own name,

began receiving so much notoriety, that it was difficult for him to pull it off. Maybe his last great performance was his United Nations caper.

In 1948 Stanley actually got a legitimate job as a journalist with the Irwin News Service. He was assigned to the United Nations, which at that time assembled at Lake Success. Stanley was a good journalist, but soon he was overcome by that old urge to be bigger and better.

While covering the United Nations, he became great friends with many of the delegates, one of whom was Ambassador Wan Waithayakon of Thailand. Stan suggested that he could help the Ambassador and Thailand if he could be appointed Special Public Relations Counsellor with diplomatic status. The ambassador thought it a great idea. While being cleared for diplomatic status, the F.B.I. uncovered the dapper con man. Stan had come within an ace of becoming an honest to goodness diplomat.

In August 1960, Stan was employed as the night clerk in a New York hotel. One night two armed men walked into the hotel and demanded the cash box he was about to put in the safe. He refused to hand it over. One of the men lunged for the box. Stanley could have let go and the men would have fled. We will never know what went through his mind during those few seconds. All the roles he had played, all the fun he had had—now, if there was ever to be meaning to his life, would he grasp the chance? This was no role, it was real.

Later, Stanley Weyman's body was found riddled with bullets on the floor of the hotel. The cash box lay intact beside him.

PART 4

POT POURRI

THE WHITE WITCH OF ROSEHALL

Over the years we have travelled some strange paths together, searching out authentic new crimes. From the fogbound streets of London, England, to the art museums of Holland, and deep into the Canadian bush, the dastardly acts of abnormal characters have led us a merry chase.

Come along with me now to Jamaica. It sounds far away and, in fact, is over 2,000 miles from Toronto; but with today's jets you can land in Montego Bay three hours and 50 minutes after takeoff from Toronto.

When Christopher Columbus landed in Jamaica in 1494, in one of those boats whose name you had to memorize in school, he stated that he thought Jamaica was the fairest land in all the world. Nearly 500 years later, no one has ever argued with Mr. Columbus' opinion. Jamaica is beautiful.

As I write this the temperature is hovering between 83 and 85 degrees F. The Jamaicans, who are amongst the friendliest people I have ever met, are quick to point out that it is now winter. In summer it is between 7 and 10 degrees warmer, and it simply never gets cold.

* * *

A few miles from Montego Bay, off the main road up a slight rise, stands a restored house called Rose Hall, which was once a stately home on a flourishing plantation. The owner's house on a plantation is by far the most impressive, and is always referred to as the Great House.

In 1964 John Rollins, an American industrialist, purchased the plantation, which was in a state of ruin, and commenced to restore Rose Hall to its 18th and 19th century elegance. His wife, Linda, has travelled the world to furnish the Great

House with antiques which duplicate those contained in the old home when it was the centre of a turbulent plantation consisting of thousands of acres of land and worked by hundreds of slaves.

In 1746 Henry Fanning purchased the plantation, which was comprised of 290 acres of sugar cane land. Fanning took a wife, Rosa Kelly, and then promptly died of natural causes. Rosa proved to be hard on husbands. In the next 20 years she went through three more, each of whom left her better off financially when they died. Her fourth and last husband was the Hon. John Palmer, who owned the adjoining plantation, Palmyra. It was he who built Rose Hall between 1770 and 1780, the finest home in all Jamaica.

In 1821, the plantation passed by inheritance to Palmer's great-nephew, John. In this way he became owner of the now huge 6,600 acre plantation. John took as his bride a rare beauty, Annie Patterson. Annie had been raised by a voodoo priestess in Haiti, and married John shortly after arriving in Kingston, Jamaica. A petite young girl of 18, all the old records describing her appearance emphasize her chalk white skin and her contrasting long black hair. Friend and enemy alike recognized her as an extremely beautiful woman.

And now to fully comprehend the story of Annie Palmer, we must almost shut out everything we think of today as being normal social behavior. In Annie's day plantation life was dominated by its labor supply, and that labor was supplied by slaves.

The social order of all plantation life was vertical. At the apex was the Great House. The next most imposing structure at Rose Hall was the residence of Mr. John Ashman, the overseer. Everyone, other than the owner, was answerable to the overseer, including the handful of whites who acted as accountants, foremen, and other skilled labor. At the bottom of the social ladder, and the most numerous by far, were the slaves. All were black, and all had nothing except what was doled out to them to keep them alive. With the temperature ranging between 80 and 100 degrees, cutting sugar cane and distilling rum was hot, backbreaking work.

Annie Palmer immediately asserted herself as the real master of Rose Hall. She accomplished this by poisoning her husband, John Palmer. He died in his upstairs bedroom. As my charming Jamaican guide, Deleta Kemble said, "It was right in this very room that she fed him deadly African beans, crushed and mixed in milk."

The woman who was to become known as the White Witch of Rose Hall was now the owner of one of the great plantations in Jamaica. Annie ruled her domain like a dictator. Each day she left the house only once when the sun was up and that was to supervise the whipping of her slaves in her back yard. Men and women alike were stripped naked and flogged in front of Annie. Many times she wouldn't give the order to stop and the slaves died tied to the whipping post. The slaves came to believe that she could cast voodoo spells. Some old records hint that using the power of suggestion she conjured up apparitions.

To add to the slaves' fear, she kept a torture chamber under the house. Of course, here in Jamaica, there are those who, even today, say that Annie Palmer was a bona fide witch of the devil.

At night she would don men's clothing, and dressed in black, astride a galloping horse, she would roam her vast estate. What horror must have filled the mind of a slave who Annie stumbled upon during her nocturnal wanderings. Annie was above all a passionate female, who sometimes took a slave as a lover. Her erratic and eventful life at Rose Hall continued. It is reported that when she tired of one lover, she did away with him by pouring boiling oil in his ear as he slept. Another was pushed through the upstairs sitting room window of the Great House.

Annie was to take two additional husbands, both of whom fared no better than John Palmer. One she strangled to death with the aid of a slave, and the third was stabbed to death in his bedroom. During the restoration of this bedroom bloodstains were found on the wall under a layer of wallpaper.

Robert Rutherford arrived at Rose Hall from England to take up his duties as bookkeeper on the planation. Known only to himself, he had another purpose for being in Jamaica. His father had inherited a plantation in Barbados. Young Robert was to observe and learn how a plantation was run, and later take over his father's operation. Thus Robert did not have the innate fear of being left without a job in a strange land, if he incurred the displeasure of the overseer, Mr. Ashman.

Within a few hours of his arrival at Rose Hall, Robert was told that it was quite normal for him to be issued a slave as housekeeper, who would cook his food and wash his clothing. She would also act as his lover. In the subculture that was slavery, if you had a kind and attractive master, this type of position was considered to be very desirable. Also vying for these preferred positions were a handful of free women who lived off the estate, but were allowed to move in under certain conditions. In this way Robert met Millicent, a perfectly proportioned, statuesque black girl. Millicent liked Robert, but he was still not wise in the ways of the tropics and accepted her for her household duties only. He refused her offers of intimacy.

Within a matter of days Robert met the mistress of Rose Hall—Annie Palmer. He couldn't believe that this beautiful, petite woman was the feared witch of Rose Hall. Annie was at once attracted to Robert, and almost immediately the pair became lovers. Their torrid romance had to resist a multitude of external influences. The overseer Ashman had been Annie's lover before Robert came on the scene. He seethed with jealousy when Robert took his place in Annie's bed. Robert was enthralled with the beauty and passion of his lover, but was unable to reconcile her treatment of him with the harsh treatment of the slaves, and the rumors about her three deceased husbands. Both Millicent and Annie, in her way, dearly loved Robert. He could resist Millicent no longer and succumbed to her charms, so that we now find him with two lovers, one white and one black.

In the society in which slavery flourished, this situation could not exist for long, for Millicent was not an ordinary member of plantation life. To fully comprehend her rather unique position one must realize that the slaves brought many of their tribal beliefs with them from Africa. The practice of Obeah or witchcraft was the most powerful of these beliefs. An Obeah man had unlimited power. By using blood, bones, feathers, and other symbols, the Obeah man could inflict a curse which could cause sickness and even death. The slaves believed in witchcraft to such an extent that if a curse was inflicted they actually became ill. There are recorded cases where deaths have been attributed to these curses.

Millicent was very special indeed, for she was the granddaughter of Takoo, an Obeah man. Annie Palmer, who had been raised by a voodoo priestess in Haiti, was also said to have Obeah powers. Robert Rutherford was sleeping with two very influential women.

One night Annie, who suspected that Millicent was more than just a housekeeper to Robert, surprised her lover and Millicent in bed in Robert's quarters. A quarrel ensued, and Millicent told Annie in no uncertain terms that Robert was her man. She insinuated that she was a better woman than Annie. No one had ever spoken to the mistress of Rose Hall in that manner before. Millicent was ordered off the plantation. She fled to the home of her grandfather, Takoo.

That night Annie Palmer went to Takoo's home and hung the small bloodsmeared skull of a child on the door of the house. A deadly curse had been placed on Millicent. Next day, after the discovery of the skull Millicent grew lethargic. Soon she became ill and her breath came in gasps. Despite the incantations of her grandfather, her condition deteriorated. When Robert heard of the curse placed on Millicent he fetched a medical doctor from Montego Bay. The doctor examined the semi-conscious girl, but could find nothing that contributed to her condition. He could do nothing for her, and Millicent died.

Takoo and several slaves armed with machetes, stormed the Great House in search for Annie Palmer. Upstairs in her spacious bedroom they found Annie. The room is the same now as it was then. A hand embroidered red and white canopy covers the oversize bed. Large windows where Annie had gazed over her domain now overlook the rolling grounds and the sea. Annie's eyes filled with terror as Takoo's hands choked the life from her body. The White Witch of Rose Hall was dead.

Takoo and his men fled to the hills. John Ashman, who truly loved Annie, formed a posse and tracked them down. Takoo was strangled to death by Ashman.

Robert Rutherford, the young accountant, left Jamaica shortly after Annie's death and never returned. Annie's grave lies a few hundred yards from the Great House. Her headstone is there to this day. In a field across the road from the present estate, five tall palm trees mark the graves of Annie's three husbands, one of her lovers, and her rival, Millicent.

Strange things are still rumored to occur in the Great

House. There are those who think that Annie Palmer still stalks the halls and rooms. In 1905, one of the girls sent to clean the interior of the house fell down the stairwell, broke her neck, and died on the spot. Some Jamaicans feel the ghost of Annie may have assisted with a slight push.

The sun shone brightly as I left Rose Hall. As I went to the parking lot I glanced over my shoulder for one last look at the impressive structure. My eyes gravitated to Annie's bedroom window. I stopped short—just for an instant was a flashing white form staring down at me? Nonsense, I thought, it might have been the reflection of the sun on a mirror in her room that caught my eye. Next day I mentioned the rather strange occurrence to a Jamaican friend. "There is no mirror in Annie's room at Rose Hall," he told me.

*   *   *

STARKWEATHER'S MURDEROUS SPREE

Wanton murder is impossible to anticipate. There is very little defence against it. The difference between a traffic light turning red or green can place an innocent victim in the sights of a deranged sniper. You can cross the paths of desperate men during the commission of a robbery through no fault of your own.

When innocent people become the victims of such a murderer, the public has a natural abhorrence to the crime. We can all relate to being in the wrong place at the wrong time.

On Tuesday, Jan. 27, 1958, Charlie Starkweather, 19, visited the home of his 14-year-old girlfriend, Caril Fugate. It was a blustery gray day in Lincoln, Nebraska. Charlie had brought along his .22 rifle. He and Caril's stepfather, Marion Bartlett, had a date to go hunting. As soon as Charlie entered the house, Caril's mother, Velda, started telling Charlie that she didn't want him around the house any more. A heated argument erupted and Velda slapped Charlie in the face. Charlie retaliated by slapping his girlfriend's mother. Finally Mr. Bartlett couldn't take any more. He came at Charlie. Without any more provocation than that, Charlie Starkweather raised his .22 and calmly shot Marion Bartlett in the head. Mrs. Bartlett grabbed a knife and advanced towards Charlie. The rifle was raised a second time and Charlie shot her, again with a bullet to the head. Two and a half year old Betty Jean Bartlett started to cry. Starkweather beat her to death with the butt of his rifle.

The house became silent. Everyone but Caril and Charlie was dead.

Charlie carried Mr. Bartlett's body out to a chicken coop at the rear of the house. He dragged Mrs. Bartlett's body to an outhouse. Little Betty Jean was placed in a cardboard box and put beside her mother. Charlie cleaned the blood off the floor, and unbelievably, he and Caril settled down to watching television for a few hours. Then Charlie went out to use a phone. He called Mr. Bartlett's employer and told him that Bartlett had the flu and wouldn't be in to work for a few days. Upon returning to the house he had intercourse with Caril. Later, he was to state that he had sex with Caril every day and twice on Sunday.

The young couple stayed on in the house. In the normal course of events, people started to arrive at the front door. Caril didn't answer some callers and they went away. The more persistent were told through the door that everyone had the flu and the doctor had ordered the house placed under quarantine. For six days the two teenagers stayed in the house after the killings. Finally Caril's elderly grandmother, sensing that something was wrong, went to the police, who investigated and discovered the three bodies. Caril and Charlie had left just before the police arrived. Starkweather took Bartlett's .410 shotgun with him.

They hadn't travelled far when Charlie's car got stuck near August Meyer's farm. Charlie, who knew Meyers, walked up to the house and asked for help in getting his car out of a ditch. The farmer went into the house for his overcoat. When he came back out, according to Charlie, he had a gun. Without hesitation, Starkweather shot him in the head. They got the car out of the ditch and drove away, but it wasn't long before they were stuck again. This time young Robert Jensen and his girlfriend, Carol King, stopped to see if they could help in any way. Charlie and Caril pulled their guns on the surprised pair. They had the terrified couple drive to a deserted school a few miles from Bennet, Nebraska. Starkweather led the pair to a storm cellar. He shot young Jensen in the head, raped and stabbed Carol King and shot her in the head as well.

That night Starkweather and Fugate spent the night in the Jensen car. The next day they walked into the home of wealthy Laver Ward in Lincoln, Nebraska. A maid opened the door to the young couple. It was to be her last day of life. Mrs. Ward came downstairs in her nightclothes. Later, on some pretext, she got permission from Starkweather to go upstairs to dress. Charlie waited for her for 40 minutes, and then went upstairs to investigate. He claimed later that Mrs.

Ward was waiting for him with a rifle. He overpowered her and stabbed her to death in minutes. At 6:30 in the evening Mr. Ward arrived home. He immediately sized up the situation and instinctively knew his only chance was to attack Starkweather. He lunged at Charlie with an electric iron. Starkweather shot him in the head, and as he spun around, he was again shot in the back. The maid was then taken upstairs, tied and gagged. She was found dead of suffocation.

Charlie and Caril left the house and headed for Wyoming. They decided to change cars about 10 miles outside of Douglas, Wyoming. They hailed a passing motorist, salesman Merle Collison. In order to gain possession of his car Charlie shot him nine times.

Then Charlie's luck ran out.

As soon as he killed Collison, another motorist stopped thinking the two vehicles were having difficulties. The driver of the car, Joe Sprinkle, got out of his car. Charlie levelled a revolver at him and said, "Raise your hands, help me release the emergency brake or I'll kill you."

Out of the corner of his eye Sprinkle saw the body of Merle Collison lying on the floor of the car. He lunged for the rifle and wrestled it away from Charlie. Later he was to state that he knew instinctively that to lose this tug of war meant death. Unarmed, Charlie dashed for his car. Strictly by coincidence, Deputy Sherriff Bill Romer drove up. Caril, who had been in the dead man's car, ran to the deputy. Starkweather roared away in Collison's vehicle. The sheriff used his radio and a car driven by Douglas Police Chief Robert Ainslie took up the chase. He fired some shots at the fleeing vehicle. One bullet went through the rear window of Starkweather's car. Charlie pulled up and dashed out of the car screaming that he was bleeding. A sliver of glass from the broken window had nicked his ear.

Immediately after his capture Charlie Starkweather started to talk. He confessed to one other murder that had taken place seven weeks before his murderous spree began. It involved a gas station robbery where the owner was taken into the woods and shot to death. In all, 11 people fell to the deadly impulses of Starkweather, the last 10 in the space of two weeks.

From the beginning Charlie insisted that Caril was a hostage and had nothing to do with the actual killings. Caril also professed to be terrified of Charlie, and thought she would become a victim at any time during the killing orgy. Later Charlie, who made seven different confessions, changed his story and implicated his girlfriend stating that she was a willing lover and accomplice.

When they placed Charlie in the electric chair on June 25, 1959, his last request was to ask the guards to tighten the leather straps holding his chest and arms.

Caril's main defence was based on the fact that she was a hostage. The prosecution attorney pointed out the many times she was armed or alone and could have run away during the deadly two weeks.

In the end, she received a sentence of life imprisonment. Imprisoned at the age of 14 Caril, spent more than half her life in prison. She was twice denied parole. However, she had her sentence of life imprisonment commuted. Caril has since been granted parole.

THE BRILLIANT KILLER

Edgar Smith holds a dubious record. He spent over 14 years in the death house in New Jersey State Prison at Trenton, the longest period of time any prisoner has ever spent on Death Row in the U.S. Not only did Smith eventually save his life, he managed to gain his freedom as well. This is his remarkable story.

*   *   *

Ed Smith first saw the light of day in Hasbrouk Heights, N.J. on Feb. 8, 1934. The town, then a suburb of New York City, had a population of 5,000. When Ed was only five his parents were divorced. His mother went to work and managed to make a living to support herself, Ed, and his older brother.

In 1948 Ed's mother remarried while her youngest son completed grammar school and entered Don Bosco Preparatory School in Ramsay, N.J., a few miles from his home. Ed, who was a good student, completed his sophomore year and then transferred to Ramsey High School. The Smith family moved to Ramsey, but Ed had had enough of school. He tried to join the Marines, but couldn't enlist until he became 18 without his mother's permission. He quit school, took odd jobs, and a few days after turning 18, joined the Marines.

While in the service Ed underwent training in California and Hawaii before being shipped out to Korea. In 1954 he was discharged due to a hearing defect in his left ear.

Returning to Ramsey, Ed went through a few jobs before settling down to a responsible position as a machinist. In 1955 he met an attractive 18-year-old girl, Patricia, who soon became his wife. The young couple bought a modern house trailer for their first home. On Dec. 23, 1956, Patricia gave birth to a baby girl. The new edition to the family was her father's pride and joy.

The above facts of Ed Smith's life fit millions of young men—small town upbringing, school, service, back home to a job, a marriage, and parenthood.

On Monday evening, March 4, 1957, all the routine aspects of Ed Smith's life were to change abruptly and forever.

At precisely 7:30 p.m. Victoria Zielinski, 15, and her 13-year-old sister, Myrna, prepared to walk to Barbara and Nixon's house. Vicki was planning on studying with Barbara Mrs. Zielinski always made Myrna walk partway with Vicki. It wasn't that far. Both homes were located on Wyckoff Ave., but the seven or eight homes between the two residences were well off the road, which can best be described as lonesome. The two sisters parted and made a deal that Myrna would leave her house at 8:30, the same time as Vicki. They would meet at the halfway point for the return walk home.

Vicki and Barbara did some homework and listened to the radio. Before Vicki realized it the time was 8:40. She hurriedly put on her coat and dashed out into the chill March air to meet her sister. Meanwhile Myrna had left home at 8:30 as arranged and was puzzled that she didn't meet Vicki. She kept walking to the Nixon residence. Barbara was surprised to see Myrna. How come she hadn't met Vicki? There was one possibility. In the few moments before the two sisters should have met on the darkened street, Vicki may have accepted a ride from a friend. Myrna returned home, but Vicki wasn't there. Mrs. Zielinski came up with a logical solution to what was fast becoming a minor mystery. The Zielinski's eldest daughter, Mary, had gone out with her steady boyfriend, George Self. Perhaps they had picked Vicki up and taken her along to one of the several teenage hangouts in town.

Myrna persisted. The only car she had seen on her walk was Don Hommell's, speeding down the road. In the meantime, feeling that Vicki would show up at any moment, Mrs. Zielinski was hesitant to wake her husband from his evening nap. When Mary and George returned without Vicki she quickly changed her mind. Mr. Zielinski was furious that his wife had not told him of their daughter's absence sooner. Three and a half hours had elapsed.

Mr. Zielinski and Mary got in their car and proceeded to look for the missing girl. During the course of the evening they met a patrol car and reported Vicki missing to the police. Throughout the wee hours of the morning the anxious father drove up and down the deserted streets. Finally he went home to try to catch some sleep.

Early the next morning Mr. and Mrs. Zielinski continued their search. A few streets removed from Wyckoff Ave., in the adjoining township of Mahwah, they entered a sandpit which ran off Chapel Rd. As they peered down the road, Mr. Zielinski spotted a shoe, which he immediately recognized as belonging to his daughter. Seven yards further down the road leading to the sandpit he found a bloodstained kerchief. Still further on he came across a pair of red gloves. Mrs. Zielinski ran to the nearest house and called the police. She returned to her husband. Not daring to proceed further, the Zielinskis waited in the car for the police to arrive.

Capt. Edmund Wickham of the Mahwah police arrived on the scene a few minutes after receiving the call. Accompanied by Mr. Zielinski they proceeded further into the sandpit area. It was Mr. Zielinski who found his daughter's body. A portion of the girl's head was nothing but a large cavity. Her brains were splattered over some nearby rocks. Vicki's brassiere was hanging loose around her waist. A post mortem later indicated that Vicki had died a virgin.

The day following the murder Ed Smith's best friend, Joseph Gilroy, was getting out of his car when he noticed a small but distinctive spot of blood on the front seat. Joe went to the police. He had loaned the car to Ed Smith the night before. Joe explained to the police that Ed's car was in the garage for repairs. Ed had needed some kerosene in order to fix the heater in his house trailer. Ed drove Joe home and took his car at about 7 p.m. He was supposed to get together with Joe later that night but called at 9:30 to say that he had been sick. He also asked if Joe would drive him and his family to his mother-in-law's house. Joe agreed. During the course of the drive Ed mentioned that he had vomited on his pants earlier that night and had thrown them away. Joe had been with Ed, his wife and baby at 9:45 p.m. and had dropped them off at his mother-in-law's at about 10 o'clock.

Next day when Joe picked up Ed at his mother-in-law's, Ed was carrying an old pair of shoes. Later during the day he no longer had them.

After hearing Joe Gilroy's story, detectives picked up Ed Smith and took him to the Mahwah police headquarters for questioning. Ed told a straightforward story of borrowing the car to pick up kerosene for his broken heater. He said that at one point he got sick and drove onto the road leading to the sandpit to vomit. Ed claimed that he returned home, but couldn't repair the heater. He then picked up Joe Gilroy for the trip to his mother-in-law's at about 9:30 p.m.

Ed explained away the old pair of shoes by stating that since his shoemaker thought they weren't worth repairing he threw them in some garbage cans in Ramsey. Police took Ed for a ride. They couldn't find his pants where he said he had thrown them, nor could they find the location where he supposedly had been sick. They did find his shoes exactly where he said they would be. One shoe had a tiny spot of blood on its side.

The interrogation continued. A physical examination revealed that Smith had abrasions on both knees. Now a prime suspect in the murder of Vicki Zielinski, police had established the following facts: 1. Ed was driving a car on the night of the murder which was later found to have a bloodstain on the front seat. 2. He lived one mile from the murder scene. 3. He was at the murder scene on the night of the murder. 4. He threw away the pants he was wearing on the night of the murder and couldn't explain where he had thrown them. 5. He threw away his shoes, which were later found with a bloodstain on one of them.

One glaring inconsistency shone through this maze of circumstantial evidence. The doctor who had examined the dead girl estimated the time of death to be not much before 11 p.m. Ed was with Joe Gilroy, his wife, baby and later his mother-in-law from about 9:45 p.m. on.

Although Ed repeatedly requested a lawyer he was refused one. At no time was he warned that he could remain silent should he choose to do so.

Detectives continued to question Ed Smith hour after weary hour. Finally, bone tired, he agreed to tell the officers exactly what happened on the night Vicki Zielinski met her death.

After picking up a five gallon tin of kerosene and starting for home, Ed claimed that he had seen a girl walking on the crowded street. He recognized her as Vicki Zielinski, whom he knew well. Ed pulled over to the side of the road and Vicki asked him for a lift to her home. The time was 8:40 p.m.

As Ed approached her home Vicki said that her sister was supposed to meet her, and that he had better drive around the block. The family didn't like her accepting lifts. Ed pulled into the sandpit road. Vicki was chatting about schoolwork and how strict her father was with her.

Suddenly Vicki turned on Ed, saying he was just like the rest of the boys she knew. She quickly informed him that she was getting out of the car and walking home. As she stepped out of the car Ed grabbed her by the shoulder. At the same time Vicki slapped him. He swung at the girl with his right hand. Vicki managed to get out of the car while Ed grappled with her. One of his shoes came off in the soft mud. He then climbed back into the car and drove home alone.

When he arrived at his trailer home he told his wife that he had been sick and threw his soiled pants on the patio. She fetched him a clean pair. Noticing that he was only wearing one shoe, he changed into a pair of loafers. Ed claimed that he then tried to repair his heater, but found that it wouldn't work.

In order to pour kerosene into a retaining tank, it was necessary for Ed to climb up on a plank superstructure and balance himself while he poured. While doing this he lost his balance and fell, skinning both his knees. This conveniently accounted for his badly skinned knees which the police were so delighted to photograph.

As Ed still had Joe Gilroy's car, he called Joe on the telephone and asked Joe to give him and his wife a lift to his mother-in-law's home in Ridgewood. Gilroy agreed. Ed gathered up his old soiled pants and drove over to pick up Gilroy. On the way he threw away his pants and then returned to the sandpit to retrieve the shoe he had left there earlier in the evening. As luck would have it, he had no trouble finding the shoe. He and Gilroy returned to the trailer, picked up Smith's wife and baby and proceeded to his mother-in-law's, where the family spent the night.

Next morning Vicki Zielinski's body was found. The murder was big news in New Jersey. Radio stations issued special reports detailing the progress of the investigation. As soon as Smith was picked up he became a prime suspect. As the questioning continued the details of his interrogation appeared almost simultaneously in the newspapers. Smith's pants were found. They were splattered with blood on the lower right leg. Ed Smith alternately claimed that he couldn't remember how they became bloodstained, or that he didn't think they were his pants. Ed claimed that he threw the pants away on Pulis Ave. They were found some distance away on Oak St. No one, including the police, could figure out how the incriminating trousers got to where they were found.

Ed's entire statement made to the police was full of evasive and unsatisfactory answers. Many questions were answered by, "I don't know" or "I can't remember". Later he was to claim that the statement was squeezed out of him in return for a promise that he would be permitted a visit from his wife.

Throughout the questioning, no lawyer was made available to Ed, despite his repeated requests for one. His statement was typed up and presented to him for his signature. He refused to sign, insisting that the police had told him beforehand that it would not be necessary for him to sign the statement. He was then asked to read the statement and initial each page. Again he refused.

After 19 straight hours of questioning Ed was permitted a visit from his wife. As one can well imagine young Patricia Smith was distraught. Newspapers carried front page stories of the heinous crime perpetrated in the small town. All the reports said that her husband had confessed to the murder. Ed assured his wife that the newspapers were wrong. He was in a jam, but the whole thing would be straightened out. They would soon be together again, just like old times. She left the police station not knowing that she would never see her husband as a free man again.

On March 6, at 7:15 p.m., Ed Smith was charged with the murder of Victoria Zielinski. He was then allowed to sleep.

Ed's first contact with the legal profession did not go off well. His lawyer met with the state attorney and elicited an agreement that his client would be allowed to plead guilty to second degree murder. The condition of the deal would be a confession given by the defendant in court from the witness stand. In this way his lawyer assured Ed that he would be a free man in eight to 10 years. Smith refused to consider the deal, and as a result his lawyer removed himself from the case.

A month after the murder Ed Smith met veteran lawyer John E. Selser, who had been retained by Smith's family to represent him. Selser was amazed to learn just how ignorant his client claimed to be concerning the murder of Vicki Zielinski. Ed inquired about the exact cause of death. While he had heard that the victim had been killed as the result of a fractured skull, he hadn't had access to a radio or newspapers, and now he wanted information about the actual murder.

For the first time Ed Smith let a fellow human being in on a secret, something he hadn't told police despite their hours of questioning. He hadn't even told his wife. Smith told his lawyer that he didn't murder Vicki Zielinski. There was more, much more. Ed knew who had killed Vicki. He had been in the sandpit at the time and had left the girl with her killer.

Ed had initially lied to the police to remove himself from the murder scene. As the questioning continued and fatigue set in he decided to lie about any detail which appeared to be advantageous to him. He didn't realize it, but with every word he was incriminating himself further.

Neither John Selser nor Ed Smith knew it at the time, but it would take over 14 years to undo the damage caused by these lies.

Edgar Smith changed his story. He now claimed to be telling the truth. It is a story he was to stick to for more than 14 years.

Smith claimed that on the night of the murder he was driving home with a five gallon can of kerosene when he picked up Vicki, who asked him for a lift to her home down the road. Once in the car Vicki, whom he knew quite well, said she had something to tell him. He pulled into the sandpit road and turned off the ignition. Vicki then informed him that his wife Patricia was seeing one of his friends on the sly. Initially Ed shrugged off the inference as being ridiculous, but as Vicki insisted on pressing the matter he became angry. In a blind rage he slapped the girl. Vicki opened the car door and ran toward the street. Ed decided to back the car down the road, at the same time trying to make up his mind whether or not he should catch up to Vicki, apologize for losing his temper and take her home.

As this thought was going through his mind he heard two

voices, one male and one female, coming from further down the road. Ed applied the brakes. Not knowing what to expect in the darkened sandpit Ed took with him a baseball bat which had been lying on the back seat of Gilroy's car. In getting out of the car he slipped in soft mud and lost his shoe. As he approached the two agitated figures, he noticed a car parked on the street at the intersection to the sandpit. He recognized the car as belonging to an acquaintance of his, Ed Hommell.

Vicki was crying. She had a nasty head wound which was bleeding profusely. Hommell, who was somewhat of a regular boyfriend of Vicki's, was berating her for having parked with Ed Smith. Vicki was obviously afraid of Hommell and asked Ed to take her home. Hommell explained to Smith that Vicki had fallen and cut her head.

Smith claimed that he offered to take the girl to a doctor. With this suggestion Vicki jumped into his car. Hommell then flew into a rage and grabbed Vicki by the arm, pulling her out of the car. Vicki grabbed Smith's legs as the upper portion of her body fell out of the car. She held tight to his legs as he stood beside the car. In this way Smith's pants, particularly the right leg, became bloodstained. During the commotion Smith had discarded the baseball bat. Hommell and Smith began shoving each other, but in a moment it was all over. Vicki got to her feet. Hommell said he would take care of the bad cut on his girlfriend's head. Everyone seemed to make up after a fashion. Edgar Smith departed, leaving Vicki and Hommell alone on the sandpit road. The baseball bat was forgotten.

After arriving home Smith discarded his bloody pants and tried to repair his space heater. He fell down while pouring kerosene into a retaining tank and skinned his knees. Later, he threw away his bloody pants and returned to the sandpit to retrieve his shoe. He found the shoe without any trouble and observed no one on the sandpit road. He did notice Joe Gilroy's baseball bat. It was split beyond repair. Ed gave this little mystery some thought and came to the conclusion that the bat was worthless, and that Hommell had broken it on purpose in a fit of rage or in an act of spite. Hommell did have a local reputation for being a bad actor when antagonized.

Why didn't Edgar Smith tell this supposedly truthful tale

to the police instead of fabricating a confession punctuated with evasive answers. Ed had good reason. The next day after Vicki's body was found, Hommell supposedly had threatened to kill Smith's wife and child if he ever told the true story of meeting him and leaving him alone with Vicki in the sandpit on the night of her murder. Besides, once the doctor announced that Vicki couldn't have met her death much before 11 p.m., he knew he would be cleared. He had several witnesses, including Joe Gilroy, who would swear that he was with them from 9 p.m. on.

What happened to the split baseball bat, which Smith claimed to have left in full view in the sandpit? It was later found a short distance away in some woods. How did it get there? Did the real killer return after Smith's trip to pick up his shoe? Did the real killer attempt to hide the murder weapon? It hardly seems plausible that if Smith were guilty he would return to the sandpit to pick up a shoe.

On May 13, 1957 Edgar Smith stood trial for the murder of Vicki Zielinski. At the conclusion of the trial the jury took only two hours and 20 minutes to find Smith guilty. A week later he was sentenced to death in the electric chair.

Whatever else Edgar Smith may be, he has never been accused of being dull. Once in the death house he began his struggle to stay alive. Appeal followed appeal over the next 14 years. In all 19 appeals were filed proclaiming his innocence.

Smith accomplished more during his 14 years on death row than he ever did on the outside. To facilitate his struggle he studied law. Many of his legal efforts have been lauded as the equal of anything produced by experienced lawyers. To help finance his legal endeavors, he wrote three books while on death row, all of which sold briskly. Tested by Mensa, an organization which only accepts individuals with extraordinary intelligence quotients, it was discovered that Smith had outstanding mental capacities. He became a member of Mensa.

Smith's gallant struggle to prove his innocence captured the imagination of journalist William F. Buckley. He believed implicitly in Smith's innocence. Buckley was instrumental in raising funds to further help Smith's continual legal moves to stay alive and eventually prove his innocence.

As the years passed, and appeal after appeal was turned

down, it became increasingly evident that pursuing a new trial on technical grounds was impractical. Smith had now been on death row for 14 years, longer than anyone in U.S. history. Caryl Chessman had held this dubious record before being put to death in San Quentin's gas chamber, after spending over 11 years in the death house.

A deal was struck. Smith went through the charade of admitting his guilt in return for a sentence of from 25 to 30 years in prison. Because of his complete and outstanding rehabilitation, the sentence was reduced to time already spent in prison. Smith was released. The battle was over. The victory wasn't sweet, but the electric chair had been cheated. Edgar Smith was free.

News conferences and television talk show interviews followed. Alert, bright, mature, and obviously a man imprisoned by overzealous law enforcement officers, Smith had at last gained his liberty.

*   *   *

Five years after Edgar Smith's release from the death house Mrs. Lefteriya Ozbun was kidnapped from a San Diego, California parking lot. Her kidnapper forced her into a car at knifepoint. The terrified woman struggled with the man and was stabbed during a wild ride on the freeway. Mrs. Ozbun managed to get away and her attacker escaped.

Later, the now 43-year-old Edgar Smith returned to San Diego and surrendered to authorities. He confessed to kidnapping Mrs. Ozbun. In his own words he intended to "tape her up and rob her." Why had he turned himself in? Smith explained that after the kidnapping of Mrs. Ozbun he had visited the grave of Vicki Zielinski in Honesdale, Pa. It was then he decided to turn himself in. "I recognized the devil I had been looking at in the mirror for 43 years was me, and I admitted what I was. I never admitted the truth to anyone, not even myself. I didn't want to believe I am what I am."

Charged with kidnapping with attempt to rob and attempted murder, Smith testified about the 25-year-old Zielinski murder. "I knew her for a year. She dated my friends and she led me to believe she would not mind seeing me." ... "I gave her a ride and we had some preliminary sexual activity, and there came a point when she resisted. I struck her a couple of times in the car. She got out."

Smith said he chased the girl with the baseball bat, caught up to her and clubbed her to death. He described his celebrated 14-year struggle to gain his freedom as nothing more than "judicial theatrics".

In 1977 Edgar Smith was found guilty of the charges pertaining to the Ozbun crimes. He was sentenced to life imprisonment without possibility of parole.

MAD MADAME WEBER

In all the annals of crime, perhaps no case has been as baffling as the Jeanne Weber case. Not because Madame Weber was a master criminal, but because her crimes were so horrible that medical doctors did not want to believe the truth.

Jeanne was born in 1875 in the fishing village of Côtes-du-Nord, France. She left home at the age of 14, and wandered throughout the country. Jeanne existed by taking odd jobs before moving on to another village or town.

By 1893 she was a not too attractive slum dweller in Paris. But all was not doom and gloom for Jean, for around this time in her life she met Marcel Weber. Soon the pair married, and Jeanne moved in with her husband and a host of in-laws. in-laws.

The young couple produced three children, and while any marriage that is confined to the slums of Paris cannot be described as delightful, the Webers seemed to be relatively happy. Their happiness was shortlived. Tragedy struck the household when their two youngest daughters died of natural causes. Jeanne took their deaths hard. She began to join her husband in drinking bouts, and it wasn't long before her consumption exceeded his ample capacity. When not into the sauce, Jeanne kept to herself, and suffered from long spells of depression.

Thrown together with her in-laws, she was often given the task of taking care of her nieces and nephews. One fine day in March, one of her sisters-in-law asked Jeanne to babysit her two daughters, Georgette and Suzanne, while she took her laundry to the local wash house. Jeanne obliged and went to her sister-in-law's apartment in Rue Pré-Maudit.

A neighbor, Madame Pouche, was walking by the open door of the apartment and saw Georgette on Jeanne's lap. It appeared to her that the child's face was turning blue. She ran and fetched Jeanne's sister-in-law from the washhouse. When they arrived back at the apartment they found Jeanne massaging the child's chest. Georgette recovered from what seemed to be a convulsion. The mother thanked Jeanne for her quick reaction to the emergency, and went back to the washhouse.

Within an hour Pierre Weber, the child's father, arrived home to find his daughter dead. Her face was blue, and it was obvious that she had gone into convulsions a second time. Apparently, this time Jeanne was unable to save her. Madame Pouche, who was again at the scene, mentioned the strange discoloration on the child's neck, but no one paid any attention to her. When a doctor arrived she mentioned the markings to him, but he too, dismissed her probing inquiries.

Nine days later, the unsuspecting mother left her other daughter, Suzanne, with Jeanne while the family went shopping. When they returned, Suzanne was dead. Again, Madame Pouche pointed out the strange markings on the child's throat. To appease the talkative woman, the doctor informed the police. A gendarme arrived and did a cursory investigation. He believed that the child could have received the marks while convulsing, and stated that he found no evidence that Suzanne had died of anything but natural causes. He further stated that it was apparent convulsions ran in the family—hadn't they recently lost another daughter in exactly the same way? "A tragedy," he exclaimed, and probed no further.

Two weeks later, another sister-in-law, left her seven-month-old daughter, Germaine, with Jeanne. When she returned from a shopping trip she found Jeanne massaging little Germaine's chest. It seems she had convulsed while her mother was out. Luckily the child recovered. Much relieved, the mother again went shopping—this time when she returned her daughter was dead. That same night Jeanne's one remaining child, Marcel, died of suffocation in his sleep.

Up to this point no serious suspicion was cast upon Jeanne. It boggles the imagination to fathom how this could be so, but one must remember that our pleasant little narrative took place in the slums of Paris at the turn of the century. There was a high mortality rate among children. Diptheria often raged through the slums leaving hundreds of children dead. Diagnoses were casual and often ambiguous.

Yet another sister-in-law left her one year old son, Maurice, in Jeanne's care. She returned unexpectedly a few minutes later to find Maurice blue in the face and gasping for breath. She accused Jeanne of choking the child. Then she gathered up her son and rushed him to the emergency ward of the Bretonneau Hospital. In the course of treatment the doctor discovered tell-tale red marks on the child's throat. He stated that the marks were caused by attempted asphyxiation. Jeanne's sister-in-law was justifiably furious. She went to the police and related the history of death that seemed to follow Jeanne.

On this information, Jeanne was later arrested. Doctors examined young Maurice's throat, but there were no visible marks left by the time the examination was performed. Some of the bodies of the young victims were exhumed. No distinct conclusion could be reached which pointed to manual strangulation as the cause of death. Despite this, the authorities were so convinced of Jeanne's guilt that they proceeded to commit her to trial for murder. No matter what else she may have been, Jeanne was no fool. She kept her mouth shut, hired a good lawyer, and was acquitted.

Nothing was heard of Jeanne (who was now being referred to in the press as L'Ogresse) for over a year. Then, in a small village in central France, a nine-year-old youngster, Auguste Bavouzet, was found dead under mysterious circumstances. There was discoloration about the throat, but after examination by the family doctor, it was decided that the child had died of natural causes. Auguste's older sister didn't believe the doctor. In fact she was extremely suspicious of the family's new housekeeper, Madame Moulenet. She was so suspicous that she secretly searched the housekeeper's belongings. She found newspaper clippings and photographs revealing that Madame Moulenet was none other than Jeanne Weber.

The sister rushed to the police with this startling information and an expert pathologist was brought in to examine Auguste's body. He stated the cause of death was strangulation. Jeanne was arrested again and caused some embarrassment to the doctors who had examined her other victims. Despite the overwhelming series of coincidences that put one woman at the scene of so many similar deaths, these doctors continued to maintain that they had been right in their original diagnoses as to the cause of death of the earlier victims.

At Jeanne's trial these same doctors were called upon to testify. Auguste's body was exhumed, and the doctors claimed that the cause of death was typhoid fever. The press and the public alike declared that Jeanne was a mass murderer. Unbelievably, once more, she walked out of court a free woman.

In May, 1908, Jeanne was up to her old tricks. She was now living in a rented room as the wife of a man named Bouchery. One night Bouchery's employment necessitated his staying out all night. Madame Bouchery asked her landlord, Monsieur Poirot, if his seven-year-old son Marcel, could stay overnight with her for company. You guessed it—that night the whole house was awakened by the child's screams. When they rushed into the room they actually found Madame Bouchery in the act of strangling the boy. A doctor was summoned to the scene and readily identified thumb and finger imprints on the child's neck. A check by the police revealed that Madame Bouchery was our friend Jeanne.

In October, 1908, Jeanne was declared insane and was confined to a home for the mentally ill. She was a violent patient and was kept in close confinement for two years. Then Jeanne once more did what she had so much practice doing—she firmly clamped both her hands against her throat and succeeded in choking herself to death.

THE CANDY MOSSLER CASE

It has been said that no millionaire has ever been executed in the United States. Candy Mossler almost became the exception to the rule.

Born Candace Weatherby in Buchanan, Georgia, in 1919, she was the sixth of 10 children. Her father was a not-too-prosperous rancher. At the age of nine, she was crippled with polio. The dread disease left Candy with one leg completely paralysed. For five years her brothers carried her to school on their backs. By diligently exercising the leg, she was able to walk again by the time she was 14. Everyone agrees that Candy was a bright, beautiful child who was soon to blossom into an extremely attractive young lady.

Candy left school in Grade 11 to marry Norman Johnson, a civil engineer. The young couple had two children, Norman, Jr., and Rita. Later they had an amicable divorce, and remained good friends. After the split-up, Candy went to New York where she became a successful model. By 1949 she was in business for herself, and profitably ran the Candace Finishing School, Candace Modelling School, and the Candace Model Agency. She was so successful that she had the resources and ability to take part in charitable causes. It was while soliciting funds for worthy causes that she met Jacques Mossler, who had just lost half of his fortune through a divorce. He had four children, and four finance companies. Jacques was down to his last million when he met Candy. He fell hard for the blonde beauty. Despite being over 20 years her senior, he married Candy on May 24, 1949 in Fort Lauderdale, Florida.

The Mosslers were devoted to each other, worked hard at the finance business, and branched out into banking and insurance. The money poured in—they became multi-millionaires.

174

In 1957 they made national news when they adopted four children at one time. In Chicago, a psychopathic war veteran ran amuck and killed his wife and baby. The remaining four children, Martha, 6; Dan, 5; Chris, 3; and Eddie, 2, were adopted by the Mosslers and became instant millionaires.

The Mosslers and their 10 children lived like kings. Their home in Houston was a 28 room mansion with rolling formal gardens and an olympic size swimming pool. Candy received $7,500 a month to run the show, except when there was a birthday or party in the family, then she usually received an extra $5,000 for incidentals. At this time the Mossler empire included the American National Bank of South Bend, Indiana; The First National Bank of Coral Gables, Florida; The Mutual Bank of Chicago, and The Central Bank and Trust Co. of Miami. A further 35 companies were controlled by a holding company—the Mossler Acceptance Corp. We needn't go into their vast real estate and property holdings. Suffice to say, the Mosslers were loaded.

In 1961, Mossler gave a job to Candy's nephew Mel Powers, the son of one of her older sisters. By 1962 Mel was living with the family in the mansion in Houston. Later evidence was to reveal that it was around this time that the warm relationship which existed between Candy and her husband began to cool. Candy was the first to drop the hint that she thought her husband had acquired homosexual tendencies at this time. Still, to all outward appearances, they had the ideal marriage.

Mossler, who was later suspected of many things, was never accused of being dumb. In June of 1963, he fired Mel Powers and had him removed from his home in Houston. Harsh words were exchanged between Mossler and Powers. Because of the convenience and mounting business interest, Mossler rented an apartment on Key Biscayne, Fla., in May of 1964. Soon the family joined him.

In the early morning hours of June 30 that year, tragedy was to descend on the Mossler clan. Candy was suffering from a migraine headache. She piled her four children into her car and took off for Miami's Jackson Memorial Hospital at about 1:30 in the morning. This may seem like strange behavior, but the family had made many excursions of a like nature in the middle of the night. They lingered, buying stamps and mailing letters on the way to the hospital. Candy received treatment at the hospital and arrived home at about 4:30 a.m. She and the children found Jacques Mossler lying on the living room floor, with a head wound and a further 39 stab wounds over his body.

The police were able to ascertain from people who lived in the apartment building that Mossler's killer had sped away in a white 1960 Chev which had been parked beside the apartment building. Later the car was found in the Miami Airport parking lot, and was traced back to Candy. It seems she was accustomed to borrowing a car any time she wanted from one of her husband's finance companies. Candy had actually taken delivery of this car days before the murder and delivered it to Mel Powers at Miami Airport.

As soon as the police got a line on Powers, other revealing tidbits started to come to light. Witnesses were found who told of a torrid affair taking place between Candy and her nephew over the past several years. Then police found out that Powers had flown from Houston to Miami the day before the murder.

Because of the wealth of those involved, the case became a celebrated one and was covered extensively by the press. It wasn't until Jan. 17, 1966 that Candy and Mel stood trial for the murder of Jacques Mossler.

During the trial four different criminals testified that they were offered the contract to kill Mossler by Powers and Candy. All flatly refused, except one who testified that he had accepted $7,500 in advance. He claimed to have spent the money without ever going through with the scheme.

The prosecution came up with Powers' palm print, lifted from the formica counter in the Mossler apartment. A handyman testified that he had washed down the counter on the afternoon preceding the murder. Thus Powers was placed in the apartment at least close to the time of the tragedy.

Perhaps the most damaging evidence of all was that of the witness who told of Powers bragging about his sexual prowess with Candy. This evidence was given in detail from the witness stand and caused the courtroom to hum. The underlying motive of the whole crime was attributed to sex.

The defence, led by famed lawyer Percy Foreman of Texas, tried to establish that there were scores of men who, for business reasons, wanted Mossler out of the way. The defense also made light of the affair between Candy and

Powers, proving that in many instances Candy's children accompanied her and Powers on supposedly illicit trips. Foreman pressed home the fact that all the evidence was circumstantial; there were no witnesses to the crime.

An all male jury brought in the surprise verdict of Not Guilty. Candy and her nephew walked out of court into the Florida sunshine.

Despite her wealth, tragedy continued to stalk the attractive blonde. In 1971, she married again. This time the groom was Barnett Garrison, an electrical contractor. About a year later he fell off the roof of their home in Houston and was seriously injured. Later Candy divorced him, and he remains a semi-invalid to this day. Melvin Powers is a successful building contractor in Houston, Texas.

On October 25, 1976 Candy flew to Florida to attend the monthly board meeting of the Central National Bank, which she controlled. The next day she didn't appear for breakfast. When she didn't respond to phone calls, officials of the Fountainebleu Hotel decided to investigate. They found her dead in her bed. She had apparently passed away peacefully in her sleep.

THE MAN WHO KILLED MARTIN LUTHER KING

James Earl Ray was born in Quincy, Ill., on March 10, 1928 to James and Lucille Ray. He was one of four children to be born to the dirt-poor family in the first seven years of their marriage. James, Sr., had been to prison for theft before his marriage, and now, with four children to feed during the worst depression the world has ever known, he took to drinking heavily. The family moved to Ewing, Missouri. Things were no better, but like everyone in the tiny hamlet of 350 souls, they did survive.

Young James started school at the Ewing Consolidated School, and is remembered as a shy, retiring youngster.

By 1943 the head of the family abandoned the farm and moved his household to Galesburg, Ill., where he got a job on the railroad. Just before they pulled up stakes, young Jimmy graduated from the eighth grade. Jimmy didn't accompany the rest of the family. Instead he struck out on his own, getting a job with a shoe manufacturing firm in Alton, Ill. In 1945, Jimmy joined the army. After serving a stint overseas, he received a discharge in 1948. Upon returning home he found his mother had given birth to two additional children. Lucille was now a confirmed alcoholic who hung around bars with strange men.

James Earl Ray left home, and from the age of 21 became a small time thief who wasn't very smart. In 1949 he was caught stealing a typewriter in Chicago, and received 90 days in jail. A few years later he was apprehended by a passing citizen as he held up a cabdriver for $11.90. He received a sentence of from one to two years in the State Penitentiary at Joliet, and was released after serving 22 months. When he got out of prison Ray went home to Alton and got a job in a gas station. A short time later, a cop making nightly routine calls along the main street of the tiny town saw a window open. As he went to investigate, a burglar rushed out the door and outdistanced the policeman. Returning to the scene the policeman found a pair of shoes stuck in the mud beside the sidewalk. Next day, James Earl Ray was picked up walking along railroad tracks on the outskirts of town. His feet were horribly swollen and bleeding. The total take from the robbery was $23. A relative posted bond, and Ray promptly skipped.

Next Ray was picked up passing forged postal orders. This time he received three years in Leavenworth, gaining his release on April 15, 1958. A little over a year later Ray received his most severe sentence. Now a four-time loser, he was sentenced to 20 years for armed robbery of a grocery store in St. Louis. After serving approximately eight years in prison, Ray escaped. On April 23, 1967 he secreted himself in a truckload of bread that was being sent from the prison proper to a prison farm close by. The truck was routinely searched but Ray had concealed himself in the middle of the load of breadboxes, and cleanly escaped, then promptly disappeared.

* * *

This, then, was James Earl Ray. To this point in his life he is one of those gray, faceless thousands who start as juvenile delinquents and progress through correctional institutions for the rest of their lives. Ray's criminal activities were planned and executed ineptly. In everything he did, he was totally incompetent.

This man, with this background, was to fire a shot and kill a man. In one split second he may have changed the course of history. In doing so he also triggered the greatest manhunt in the history of crime.

* * *

After his successful escape from prison, Ray called himself John Larry Rayns. He made his way to Chicago and got a job washing dishes at the Indian Trail Restaurant. He stayed eight weeks, got along well with the rest of the kitchen staff, and made a total of $700. On July 16, 1967 he crossed the border at Windsor, Ont. and made his way to Montreal. Two days later he took a six month lease on a room at the Har-K apartments at 2589 Notre Dame St. E. He signed the lease as Eric S. Galt. It is believed that at the time of the signing of this lease Ray was now actively involved in conjunction with others in a master conspiracy to assassinate Dr. Martin Luther King. Eric S. Galt's activities in Montreal are well documented. He paid $150 in advance for his room at the Har-K Apartments. On July 18, he bought a suit, pyjamas, gray slacks, two t-shirts, swim trunks, underwear and ties at Tip Top Tailors. Two days later he had his nails manicured at the Queen Elizabeth Hotel.

On July 31, he went to the Laurentian Mountains where he checked into a luxury resort. He stayed a week. Where did the money come from? Throughout Ray's travels, this question arises again and again. For a man with no income, money seemed to be no object in Ray's date with destiny.

Another mystery is the fact that there appears to be a marked change in Ray's personality at this time. The man who bought drinks at the bar in the Laurentian resort was not a shy hillbilly hood on the lam. Ray – Galt was now a confident, smooth talking, free spender. He even managed to bed down with a cultivated employee of the federal government. This poor lady was to be questioned extensively by the federal police of two countries because of her connection with the dapper Eric Galt.

Later, Ray – Galt was to claim that he met with a man in Montreal he was to know only as Raoul. Ray says he entered into an agreement with Raoul that he would do anything Raoul asked, but in turn would ask no questions himself. Ray claims that if he was now part of a conspiracy, he knew nothing about it. Under the auspices of the mysterious Raoul, who incidentally has never been identified, Ray – Galt travelled from Montreal to Birmingham, Ala., to Mexico, to New Orleans and Los Angeles. Contact was always made with him and money was provided to finance his travels.

In Birmingham, Ray bought a white 1966 Mustang. He answered an ad in the Birmingham News, met William D. Paisley and paid cash for the car.

This was certainly strange behavior for an escaped convict who was on a mission to murder a Nobel Peace Prize winner. Dr. Martin Luther King was a living legend to both white and black. Those who disagreed with his views still admired his courage. Those who agreed with the black leader considered him a god. All agreed that he was the one man who had any chance of unifying the various black groups in the United States. They also agreed that Dr. King had no ulterior motives. He was willing to give his life for his people.

In 1968, Dr. King had already made public his plan for a camp in Washington. The whole operation was to be called Resurrection City. On Feb. 19, in Los Angeles, Ray – Galt had some plastic surgery performed on the tip of his nose and on his left earlobe. These minor but identifiable marks were successfully removed.

Again, receiving mysterious instructions from Raoul, Ray moved from Los Angeles to Atlanta and on to Birmingham. In Birmingham, using the name Harvey Lowmeyer, Ray bought a 30.06 calibre Remington rifle with a telescopic lens. Ray then drove the white Mustang back to Atlanta, then on to Memphis.

Meanwhile, after a bomb scare on his plane, Dr. King arrived in Memphis. He was met at the airport and accompanied to the Lorraine Motel. Dr. King was assigned Room No. 306.

Using the name John Willard, Ray checked into a dilapidated boardinghouse at 422½ South Main St. The manager of the boardinghouse, Mrs. Bessie Brewer, thought her new customer too well dressed for her establishment. She showed him the best rooms in the house, but Mr. Willard didn't like the view. He thought Room No. 5b was perfect. It was filthy, had a lumpy mattress and nondescript green spread on the bed. The dirty window gave an unobstructed view of the Lorraine Motel. In his direct line of vision was Room 306.

Down the hall from his room Mr. Willard noticed that the common bathroom gave a still better view of Room 306. He entered the bathroom and locked the door. At 6 o'clock Dr. King came out of his room onto the balcony for a breath of air. John Willard stepped into the bathtub, rested his Remington on the windowsill and squeezed the trigger. Exactly 205 feet 3 inches away (the distance was later measured) Dr. King was slammed against the wall. The bullet tore into his lower right jaw and hit his spinal cord. At 5 minutes past 7 Dr. Martin Luther King was officially pronounced dead.

* * *

James Earl Ray, alias John Willard, rushed from the boardinghouse, and for some reason dropped his rifle in front of a store close by. He entered his white Mustang, and in the confusion got clean away. He made it to Atlanta in the Mustang and then abandoned it. Somehow (no one to this day knows what means he used) Ray headed for Toronto.

In his wake Ray left a nation in a state of hate. The non-violent advocate King, lay dead by an assassin's bullet. Surely, if the white man would kill the leader of the non-violent movement, could non-violence ever achieve the black man's dream of full equality? The answer came in the form of riots and fires. From Memphis, Washington, Chicago, Albany, Youngstown, Baltimore, Kansas City, Newark, and Pittsburgh, the hate, fires and rioting spread. It is estimated that damage amounted to $50 million in the one week following the murder.

The F.B.I. recovered a note left by Galt in Atlanta. On the note they discovered a fingerprint. The authorities started matching it with prints of known fugitives of the same description as Galt. On the 702nd card pulled the print was matched. The name on the card—James Earl Ray. On April 8, James Earl Ray walked up the few steps at 102 Ossington Ave., Toronto and rang the bell. There was a room for rent sign in the window. The red bricks have been painted many times since the evening Ray introduced himself to Mrs. Szpakowski as Paul Bridgman. The neighborhood is surprisingly the same now as it was then. A few doors away is the Maple Leaf Confectionery. The Portugal Tool Rental Co. has a modern sign over the front window giving evidence of the ethnic mix of the neighborhood. A potpourri of Italians, Portuguese, Spanish, and Chinese live in the area. Typical of Toronto and different from other large cities, these ethnic groups seem to be able to retain their culture and yet mix with the community at large. In this mixture of nationalities, no one noticed Paul Bridgman. Well, almost no one. One day his landlady, Mrs. Szpakowski mentioned to her husband the striking resemblance between their quiet boarder and the fellow the whole world was hunting. Her husband told her not to make a fool of herself—what would such a man be doing in their rooming house. Two days later, the reward for James Earl Ray hit $155,000.

On April 11, Ray – Bridgman got a passport photo taken at the Arcade Photo Studio on Yonge St. Five days later he entered the Kennedy Travel Agency. Ray – Bridgman said he wanted a 21-day excursion ticket to London, England, leaving on May 6 and returning on May 27. The agent, Mrs. Spencer explained that he needed a passport. The stranger said that he had no birth certificate. Next she suggested that he come up with someone who knew him for the past two years. He replied that he had just returned to Toronto after a long absence, and didn't know anyone. Mrs. Spencer had faced this problem before. There was one further thing to do to get a passport. Her customer had to swear before a notary that he was a Canadian citizen. Henry Moos, the president of the travel agency, was a notary and would do the necessary. The agency would send the application to Ottawa. Bridgman answered some further questions and gave his name as Ramon George Sneyd. It was under this name that the application for a passport was sent to Ottawa.

From Eric Starvo Galt, John Willard, Paul Bridgman to Ramon George Sneyd. Where did Ray get this assortment of names? How could he feel so safe using them for passports and freely establishing new identities? He was relatively safe because all four men existed and had the same general physical characteristics as Ray. They were all respected citizens of Scarborough, Ont. They never knew each other, and certainly had never met Ray. Somehow they had made an underworld list of safe names to use and were purchased by Ray or someone else, not by chance, because each one generally fit his description.

On April 19, with the newspapers full of the latest news of the most wanted man in the world, James Earl Ray changed rooming houses. He moved eight blocks away to 962 Dundas St. W. His new address was in the same ethnic area. Ray could still remain a faceless nonentity among thousands. Mrs. Sun Fung Loo didn't speak any English. Her new roomer paid his $9 for the week in advance with a crisp $20 bill.

On May 2, Ray picked up his ticket from Mrs. Spencer. He had applied for and received a birth certificate in the name of Sneyd. He paid $345 in cash for the ticket. Four days later he left his rooming house on Dundas St. W. He hailed a cab, and the most wanted man in the world drove up Hwy 27 (now 427) to Toronto International Airport. By 6 p.m. that evening he was on his way to London.

The F.B.I. realized the ease with which a Canadian passport could be obtained. They reasoned that Ray might try to leave the continent via Canada. The R.C.M.P. were asked to check passports issued since Ray escaped from prison. Over 218,000 had been issued. The Mounties set to work.

On May 7, Ray left London for Lisbon, Portugal. Still traveling under the name of Sneyd, he stayed in Lisbon eight days. It is speculated that a rendezvous was not kept by someone who was supposed to meet Ray. He was forced to return to London. Once back in London he checked into the Ekfield House Hotel, and stayed there until May 28, when he moved to the New Earl's Court Motel in Penywern Rd. Meanwhile the Mounties in Ottawa had been checking passports for 10 days, and finally came up with one in the name of Ramon George Sneyd that had a general description that could have fitted Ray. A phone call to Toronto verified that Ramon George Sneyd did indeed exist, but he had never applied for a passport. The police now had the information supplied by Ray in order to purchase his ticket and passport. They traced his actions and learned of his flight to London.

In London, Ray was starting to panic. Moving to another hotel did nothing to calm his nerves. He made inquiries about becoming a mercenary soldier in Africa.

Had the elaborate plot commenced to deteriorate? Was Ray now alone; the old Ray who left his shoes at the scene of a robbery?

On June 8, he checked out of his hotel and booked a flight to Brussels. By this time Scotland Yard had been alerted to be on the lookout for Ray traveling in Europe under the name of Sneyd. At 11:30 a.m. on the morning of June 8, when Ray rushed to the airport to catch his Brussels flight, Det. Sgt. Phillip F. Birch was checking passports and keeping an eye open for the name Sneyd. Dapper James Earl Ray dashed up to the booth and flashed his passport. Birch saw the wanted name. He said to the most wanted man in the world, "Would you please step into our office, Mr. Sneyd?"

* * *

On Monday, March 10, 1969, in Memphis, Tenn., Percy Foreman, Ray's defense counsel, informed the court that his client had signed a Petition for Waiver of Trial and Request for Acceptance of Plea of Guilty. This document was signed with the firm understanding that Ray's life was to be spared. He received a sentence of 99 years in prison. No one has ever been given the opportunity to inquire about a conspiracy. Did James Earl Ray act alone? Perhaps we will never know. Not long ago, his petition for leave to appeal was turned down. He remains confined in prison.

MURDER ON THE MOORS

The story you are about to read involves two of the most reprehensible criminals who ever lived. The depths to which their depraved acts plummeted have not been equalled in modern times. If the retelling of this grisly true tale cautions just one parent to the dangers of allowing their children to accompany not only strange men, but strange women, then this effort will have been worthwhile.

At 12:40 p.m. on Jan. 2, 1938, unwed Margaret Stewart gave birth to a son in Rotten Row Maternity Hospital, Glasgow, Scotland. For the first 12 years of his life foster parents brought up the lad as if he were their own child. Margaret, a waitress, visited her son Ian at every opportunity and contributed financially to his upbringing. In 1950, Margaret met Patrick Brady of Manchester. Recognizing her chance for happiness and escape from the slums of Glasgow, she married Patrick and moved to Manchester. Ian remained with his foster parents.

Ian was not your average child. There is evidence of his cruelty to animals while still in his preteens. He threw cats off five storey buildings to prove that they didn't have nine lives. Once he crucified a frog and relished the sheer agony he caused the helpless creature. Between the ages of 12 and 15 he broke into several shops and houses, getting caught more often than not. Judges were lenient with the pale, lean lad who stood before them. Each time he was apprehended he was put on probation so that he could continue his schooling.

When Ian was 15 he left school and was promptly charged with nine counts of housebreaking. His foster parents gave up. They would have nothing more to do with the problem child. He was given one more chance by another lenient magistrate, and left Glasgow to live with his mother and stepfather in Manchester. He took his stepfather's last name, becoming Ian Brady.

Ian drank, couldn't keep a job and continued to break into houses. Apprehended again in the act, he finally met a magistrate who sentenced him to two years in Borstal. On June 9, 1958 Ian was released from prison, but nothing had changed. He sometimes worked in a Manchester fruit market, but still couldn't hold a steady job. In February, 1959, Ian answered a newspaper ad for a clerical position. He got the job at Millwards Merchandise Ltd., a chemical supply company in West Gorton, Manchester. The job paid twelve pounds a week. Ian kept to himself, opened the firm's mail and filed orders. At night he read about Adolph Hitler and the Marquis de Sade.

* * *

Myra Hindley was born in 1942 on Eaton St., Gorton, in the slums of Manchester. When she was four her mother gave birth to a second daughter, Maureen. As the result of the overcrowding at Eaton St. Myra moved in with her grandmother a block down the street. She seldom saw her paratrooper father. Although her IQ was slightly above average, she was not a particularly good student. Myra left school while in her teens and drifted from job to job. Finally she managed to secure a position as a shorthand typist. The job paid 8 pounds 10 shillings a week. It was with Millwards in West Gorton. Much of her typing was for a lean, pale, rather eccentric young man who fascinated Myra. His name was Ian Brady.

We will never know what catalyst was at work in the offices of Millwards which allowed two children of the slums to meet, become infatuated with each other and ultimately to become monsters living in the guise of human beings. Make no mistake about it; monsters they were to become.

Ian introduced Myra to his library of witchcraft, sadism, and genocide. Myra was a quick learner. What Ian said was law; Myra never argued. The pair became inseparable. Myra purchased a mini-van, and since Ian didn't drive, it was she who chauffeured the pair to and from work.

Throughout the years Myra remained friendly with her

younger sister Maureen, who joined Millwards in 1963. Now that the sisters were employed under the same roof, Myra confided to Maureen that she was having an affair with Ian Brady. When Myra and her grandmother moved to Wardle Brook Ave. in Hattesley, Ian moved in with them. The elderly grandmother kept to herself and never interfered with the machinations of Myra and her live-in boyfriend.

Slowly Ian's fascination with Nazi Germany began to rub off on Myra. She became enthralled with Irma Grese, the Beast of Belsen, and tried to emulate her heroine. Evenings were spent experimenting with sexual perversions, drinking cheap wine, and wandering the countryside outside Manchester in the mini-van. On their days off Ian would indulge in his hobby, photography. Myra was a willing model, posing in the nude in every conceivable position or stance which Ian suggested.

* * *

Mrs. Sheila Kilbride gave her 12-year-old son John a peck on the cheek before he scampered off with a friend to attend the movies. The two lads left the movie theatre at 5 p.m. and wandered over to Ashton Market to see if they could perform some odd jobs for the tradesmen. It was getting late. John's friend caught a bus home. He last saw John talking to a friendly blonde lady. The lady was Myra Hindley.

Little John Kilbride never returned home. Police were notified and a comprehensive search followed. Months were to pass without the police uncovering anything approaching a clue as to what happened to the missing boy.

Ten-year-old Lesley Downey was excited this Boxing Day of 1964. Her mother had reluctantly given her permission to attend a fair being held only 200 yards from her home. Lesley was stepping out with neighborhood children. It all seemed so harmless. By 5 p.m. Mrs Jean Downey became apprehensive when little Lesley failed to return home. She called on her neighbors and was startled to find that the other children had been home for some time.

A mini-van parked ominously beside the fair grounds. Every so often the van circled the fair grounds, its occupants looking for a young girl. There's one! A little girl watched the bobbing painted heads of the wooden ponies on the merry go round. The mini-van came to an abrupt stop. A blonde woman approached the little girl and the pair began talking. It wasn't long before the blonde woman found out that the youngster had spent all her money. The blonde lady volunteered that she would be happy to pay for another ride and another after that. What 10-year-old child could resist such good fortune? Lesley Downey jumped on the wooden pony. Later she mentioned to the young lady that she'd better get home as her mother would begin to worry. The kind lady urged the child not to be concerned. She would personally give her a lift in her mini-van so she needn't be late after all. Lesley knew everything would be all right. Her mother had told her never to accept a ride with a strange man, but she had never said anything about a friendly, kind lady.

Lesley Downey jumped into the mini-van beside her new friend Myra Hindley. In the shadows in the back seat, behind the unsuspecting child lurked Ian Brady.

Lesley Downey was never seen again. A massive search was conducted by police which involved the questioning of 5,000 individuals and the distribution of 6,000 posters. Weeks turned into months, until gradually the investigation into the mystery of Lesley's disappearance wound down. Ten months after her ride in the min-van her fate was to make headlines around the world.

When Myra's younger sister Maureen married David Smith, it seemed most natural for the two couples to become close friends. Especially so since the Smiths moved into an apartment within walking distance of Myra and Ian. David Smith was not exactly lily white. He had been in several scrapes with the law and had an assault conviction on his record. David could never hold down a job for any period of time. He welcomed Ian's hospitality.

The two men were accustomed to staying up half the night drinking cheap wine, while Myra and Maureen went to bed. During one of these lengthy drinking bouts Ian broached David with the idea that they rob a bank. He told David he had been planning such a caper for years. David seemed receptive, but Ian's scheme didn't progress beyond the planning stage.

The strange double life being led by Ian Brady and Myra Hindley erupted into violence and terror on the night of Oct.

6, 1965. On that night Myra's 77-year-old grandmother took a sleeping pill at 8:30 p.m. and retired for the night. Myra and Ian cruised the streets of Manchester in her mini-van. Myra parked the vehicle near Central Station while Ian took a stroll. He soon returned with 17-year-old Edward Evans. Edward was a homosexual who had gladly accepted an invitation to return to Ian's home for a drink.

Once back at Wardle Brook Ave., Ian and Edward engaged in conversation while Myra called on her brother-in-law, David Smith. She convinced David that Ian had some miniature bottles he wanted to give away. David was delighted to accompany Myra back to her home.

Myra and David lingered in the kitchen admiring the miniature bottles. Suddenly a blood chilling scream ricocheted through the house. Myra screamed, "Dave, Dave, come and help Ian." Smith ran from the kitchen into the living room and into hell.

The only light came from a television set. In its eerie glow David saw Edward Evans, whom he didn't know, lying half on the floor and half on a couch. Blood was cascading from Edward's head onto the floor. Ian Brady stood over the fallen youngster with a bloody hatchet in his hand. As David watched in terror, Ian brought the hatchet down on Edward's head time and time again. Edward tried to crawl away from his tormentor, but with each vicious blow his actions became weaker.

Ian interrupted his murderous frenzy to nonchalantly comment to no-one in particular, "This one's taking a while to go." Then he attached an electric cord around his hapless victim's neck, and pulled until Edward Evans lay still in death.

Ian was soaked in blood. The room looked like a slaughterhouse. Myra's clothing had been splattered with blood as well. David Smith had been an audience of one to a murder which had been orchestrated just for him. Ian commented rather sheepishly, "It's the messiest one yet. Normally one blow is enough."

At Ian's urging Myra went about cleaning up the room. Ian then changed his clothing. Upstairs Myra's grandmother slept through it all. Ian solicited David's help in carrying the body upstairs to a bedroom. Myra then put on a pot of tea and, while David inwardly shuddered, she and Ian gloated over their recent victim.

At about 3 o'clock in the morning David suggested that he should head home, and was surprised when his companions bade him goodnight and let him leave. For Smith the whole evening had been unreal. He felt he had lived through a nightmare.

David Smith ran all the way home. He was so terrified of Ian and Myra that he waited three hours before he dared to sneak out of the house in order to call the police.

When detectives arrived at 16 Wardle Brook Ave. they were let in by Myra. They had been told by Smith that the living room would be spotless. A search of the back bedroom revealed the horribly mutilated body of Edward Evans trussed up in a plastic bag. Taken to a police station, Ian confessed to murder and at every opportunity tried to implicate David Smith. Three bloodstained carpets and the murder weapon were carried away by the police from the murder house. Later, a post mortem revealed that Evans had been struck 14 blows to the skull.

As police proceeded to interrogate Ian, and later Myra, it became obvious that neither of them had met Edward Evans before the night of the murder. What was their motive for luring the victim to their home to kill him? Was it possible, as it appeared to be, that the murderous pair had timed the first blow to coincide with David Smith's arrival so that he would be a witness to murder?

The house on Wardle Brook Ave. was practically dismantled in an attempt to discover further clues. The investigating officers were successful in their endeavors. They found Ian Brady's notes. On one page they came across the name John Kilbride, the little boy who had been missing for almost two years. There was more. Police discovered that Ian had checked two suitcases at Manchester's Central Station. They were recovered. They contained pornographic pictures of Myra, but more importantly there were weird photographs of the lonesome moors outside Manchester. Some of the photos showed Myra staring straight down at the moors, as if standing over a grave in mourning.

Police searched for and found the actual sites depicted in the photographs. They dug up the bodies of John Kilbride and little Lesley Downey.

The case was one of the most amazing murder cases ever uncovered anywhere. Christened the Murders on the Moors by the press, it received world wide publicity. The trial took place at historic Chester Castle on April 19, 1966. Due to the nature of the evidence it was felt that the two accused could very well be assassinated in the courtroom. When it came time for them to testify they were protected by four inch thick bullet proof glass on three sides. The pornographic pictures, the photos of the gravesites of the two children, and Brady's diary left little doubt as to the guilt of the accused pair.

One piece of evidence was so horrifying that hardened homicide detectives left the courtroom when this particular evidence was presented. Myra and Ian had lured little Lesley Downey to their home and recorded on tape her agony as they sexually abused and tortured her to death. The tape, which also had Christmas carols as background music to the horror they were inflicting on a 10-year-old child, had been discovered intact by police.

The Moors jury took only two hours and 22 minutes to find Ian Brady guilty on three separate counts of murder. He received three life sentences, while Myra received two life sentences for the murder of Downey and Evans. She received a further seven year sentence for harboring Brady in the case of Kilbride.

Ironically Ian Brady and Myra Hindley escaped the hangman's noose. A few months prior to their trial capital punishment had been abolished in England. They both remain in prison to this day.

MRS. SPRINGER SLEPT AROUND

Prominent married ladies should as a rule be extremely discreet when they take a lover. If they decide to have two lovers and a husband all at the same time, they should be downright cautious. This is the story of a lady who didn't know the meaning of discretion, and threw caution to the wind.

John W. Springer never knew what it was like to be poor for the simple reason that he had always been rich. Born in Illinois on the right side of the tracks to a wealthy and socially prominent family, he had the distinction of being elected to the Illinois House of Representatives at the rather tender age of 22.

They say money goes to money, and John was no exception. He married an extremely wealthy cattleman's daughter from Colorado, and thus ended up with money on both sides, so to speak. In order to participate in his father-in-law's many interests, he moved to Denver. John became a power in banking, real estate, and politics. He ran unsuccessfully for mayor of Denver in 1904. But not everything came up roses—John's wife took ill and died of natural causes.

A few years after Mrs. Springer's demise, John met beautiful, vivacious Isabelle Patterson of St. Louis. Isabelle had divorced her first husband. Despite this minor mar on her track record, John married the lady and brought her to Denver.

John had a rambling cattle ranch outside the city for relaxing, yodelling, and whatever. He also had a palatial home in the centre of Denver. Would you believe it, Isabelle didn't like the setup. She craved the action she had grown accustomed to as a gay divorcee in St. Louis. To pacify her, John rented a suite on the sixth floor of the aristocratic staid

193

Brown Palace Hotel in downtown Denver. Here Isabelle could entertain to her heart's content.

Into this comfortable menage came daring Tony von Phul, a nationally known balloonist. He also doubled as a wine salesman for an Eastern winery. Despite the social position she held in the community, despite her wealth, despite a rock of a hubby, Isabelle opted for sex with the dashing balloonist. In the spring of 1911, Mrs. Springer was bedding down with Tony at every opportunity. With Isabelle firmly ensconced on the sixth floor of the Brown Palace and Tony living on the fifth floor, we can only assume that the opportunities were numerous.

On occasion Tony's enterprises necessitated his taking excursions away from Isabelle's side. During these temporary absences Isabelle would write Tony little letters, the contents of which should have been coated with asbestos. They were very, very warm.

While all these dalliances were taking place on the sixth floor, John continued to invest wisely and make money. One of the new citizens of the community with whom he became friends was none other than Tony von Phul. Trusting John didn't suspect a thing.

Now, folks, we all know that there are more triangles in most hotels than there are in symphony orchestras. Sometimes these cute little arrangements carry on for years. In the celebrated Springer affair, still another actor was destined to walk upon the stage.

Frank Harold Henwood arrived in Denver in the winter of 1911. He was there to help promote a new gas company, but what was far more important, he arrived with a letter of introduction to John Springer. John liked Henwood. The pair became business associates in the gas company and saw a great deal of each other socially. One fine day John Springer introduced his friend Frank Henwood to his wife Isabelle, thereby proving once and for all that lightning certainly can and often does strike twice in the same place. Mrs. Springer promptly fell hard for Henwood.

Throughout the late winter and early spring of 1911, Henwood and the durable Isabelle were using the sixth floor often. During their many months of gallivanting on the sixth floor, the pair had the good fortune not to be concerned with von Phul, who was away in St. Louis on wine business. John

Springer, it appears, knew nothing about anything. It must be remembered that both of Mrs. Springer's lovers were on a first name basis with hubby John. They would often attend the opera or take business trips with Springer. Sometimes they were even accompanied by Isabelle.

One evening, while warming Henwood's bed, Isabelle revealed her relationship with von Phul. She told Henwood that, try as she might, von Phul would not return some rather revealing, foolish letters she had written to him. Henwood went so far as to dictate a letter to von Phul, which Isabelle copied in her own handwriting. It stated in no uncertain terms that she was finished with von Phul, and that he should do the honorable thing and return the foolish little letters and that was that.

She received a reply from von Phul telling her to get rid of Henwood. If she wouldn't do it, von Phul said he would take matters into his own hands.

On May 23, 1911, von Phul returned to Denver from his business trip. He met Frank Henwood for the first time. Naturally he took his old room on the fifth floor of the Brown Palace Hotel, which gives us the rather unlikely situation of having von Phul on the fifth floor, Henwood on the fourth, and Isabelle in her suite on the sixth. Where John Springer was is uncertain.

The adversaries met in the lobby of the hotel and started to argue. They retreated to von Phul's room, where von Phul revealed he was carrying a revolver. Henwood's reaction to this startling revelation was to announce, "Any man who carries a gun is a coward. I never carried one in my life."

Henwood pleaded with von Phul to return the incriminating letters. Von Phul slapped Henwood across the face. Again Henwood pleaded for the return of the letters. This time von Phul picked up a wooden shoe tree and struck Henwood with it across the temple, whereupon Henwood wisely left the room.

Von Phul was furious over the whole situation. He rushed up to Isabelle's suite and told her she was stupid to let Henwood come between them. Isabelle, whose affections could swing either way at the drop of a hat, said it just wasn't so. Then she ran to Henwood and told him to drop the whole matter. She told him he wasn't a match for von Phul, and no good was to come from the two of them arguing and threatening each other. Isabelle was right. She had set in motion a situation where two desperate men wanted her, and would go to any lengths to have her.

That evening John Springer dined with his wife in the Brown Palace Hotel dining room. At separate tables in the same dining room sat Tony von Phul and Frank Henwood. That night rooms were occupied on the fourth, fifth, and sixth floors by all the participants in what was to become the city of Denver's most celebrated case.

Next morning Henwood went to the police and demanded protection. The chief of police informed him that he could do nothing unless specific charges were brought against von Phul. This Henwood refused to do for fear of involving Mrs. Springer. Instead he went out and purchased a .38 calibre revolver.

That same evening Henwood took Mr. and Mrs. Springer to the opera. After the performance he dropped them off at their suite on the sixth floor, and went down to have a drink in the bar. The room was filled with prominent Denver gentlemen having a nightcap.

At about 11:30 p.m. Tony von Phul walked into the bar. Von Phul joined Henwood. A few words were exchanged. Then von Phul punched Henwood on the chin, sending him sprawling to the floor. Some say Tony made a move toward his pocket, as if to reach for a gun. Others swear von Phul contemptuously turned his back on his fallen adversary. Anyway it was Henwood, the man who only the day before proclaimed that only cowards carry guns, who drew his own gun. Henwood emptied the .38 calibre revolver in von Phul's direction. Three bullets found their mark. One hit von Phul in the shoulder. The second grazed his wrist, and the third brought him to the floor with a bullet to the groin.

Two men, who had never met any of the principals in the case, were unlucky enough to be in the wrong place at the wrong time. J. W. Atkinson, a Colorado Springs contractor, received a bullet wound in his leg; while G. E. Copeland, a businessman from Victor, Colo., took two slugs just below the knee. His revolver spent, Henwood went into the lobby of the hotel and awaited the police.

Strangely enough, no one died in the fusillade. Von Phul never lost consciousness and remained lucid throughout the ordeal. When asked about the reason for the outbreak, he made up a story about the two men becoming jealous over the attentions of a chorus girl. He refused to be taken to the hospital by ambulance. He went by cab. Next morning at 11 a.m. von Phul died from his wounds. He had not mentioned Mrs. Springer's name. Henwood also said the bone of contention between the two men had been a chorus girl.

However chivalrous the two men had tried to be, there was no way they could protect Mrs. Springer. Von Phul's belongings revealed photographs and the incriminating letters. The scandal broke, but even more startling events were just over the horizon.

G. E. Copeland, whose leg wounds were considered minor, contracted gangrene. He was operated on and died a few hours after the operation. Henwood, who was already charged with the murder of von Phul, was now charged with the murder of Copeland. Under Colorado law, if death comes as a result of another murder, the second death, no matter how accidental, becomes murder as well. A few days later, as if to add more turmoil to an already tumultuous affair, John Springer instituted divorce proceedings against his wife.

Henwood's trial was a celebrated one. No one will ever know why the district attorney chose to try Henwood for Copeland's murder rather than von Phul's. This is extremely strange, for in order to get a conviction for the murder of Copeland, the jury had to be presented with proof of the murder of von Phul.

All the dirty linen and all the nocturnal habits of Mrs. Springer were dragged through the courts. Servants and hotel employees told of the visits of the two lovers to the suite on the sixth floor. Who knows how many deaths would have resulted had von Phul remembered to bring his gun down to the bar that fateful night. He had forgotten it under his pillow.

Henwood was found guilty and was sentenced to life in prison. His lawyers appealed for a new trial. One of their main arguments was that the presiding judge, in instructing the jury, had noted that, "There is no manslaughter in this case." The Supreme Court ruled that the judge had been in error, and the case was remanded for retrial.

On May 28, 1913, Henwood's second trial for Copeland's murder began. By this time John Springer had divorced

Isabelle. He appeared as a broken man at the second trial.

Henwood was found guilty again, and this time he was sentenced to death by hanging. When all legal efforts to save his life failed, his lawyers appealed to the governor of Colorado, the last and only man who could save their client's life. At the last moment the governor commuted Henwood's sentence to life imprisonment. Henwood served 10 years in prison before being paroled. He changed his name and moved to New Mexico.

Within three months of his release a waitress filed a complaint against him for propositioning her. Henwood was returned to prison as a parole violater. He died there of natural causes in 1929.

ONCE TOO OFTEN

Many occupations are inherently dangerous. Miners risk their lives every day in pursuing their chosen profession. Fishermen are susceptible to the whims of nature. Prostitution may be the most dangerous profession of all. Many ladies who ply this oldest of trades end up in all sorts of trouble. Unfortunately, some become murder victims, but few attain the status of celebrated murder cases. The Frederick Field matter is an exception. It is unique in the annals of criminal history.

Fred was a nice guy—tall, good-looking, with black wavy hair. In 1931 he was gainfully employed with a firm of signpainters in London, England. For all intents and purposes, he should have gone through life working at his job, visiting his pub, and settling down with a faithful English wife for the rest of his life.

On Friday, Oct. 2, Fred and his foreman were instructed to inspect an empty shop the firm owned in Shaftesbury Ave., London. As they were performing this task the foreman saw what he thought was a wax dummy lying on the floor. He poked at the unsightly object, and only then discovered it was the body of a partially clad young lady.

He and Fred notified the police. The victim had a piece of clothing stuffed into her mouth and a jacket belt firmly fastened around her neck. The investigating officers recognized Norah Upchurch, a young neighborhood prostitute. Norah kept a flat on Shaftesbury Ave. to entertain her clients, but lived in Pimlico.

Questioning revealed that Fred Field had visited the empty shop the previous day to take down a "To Let" sign. Field told the police that while he was doing this, a man showed up who claimed to be the gent who had rented the premises. He requested the keys from Fred. Thinking that this was all quite natural, Fred turned the keys over to the stranger. During the course of their conversation, Fred let it be known that he was somewhat of an electrician. The stranger seemed particularly interested in the lighting of his new shop. This topic was discussed for some time. Fred was led to understand that he would be given the contract to alter the lighting system.

The pair made an appointment to meet later that night at Piccadilly Station. Fred claimed that his new friend showed up, but had forgotten the keys to the shop. He left to get the keys and never returned. Fred waited a while and then went home.

Naturally enough, the police were extremely interested in Fred's story, especially since it provided them with a detailed description of the stranger. Before you could say Robert Peel, the bobbies had picked a prime suspect for Fred's perusal. Quick as a flash, Fred identified the man as the stranger who had taken the keys to the shop where poor Norah was killed.

Everything was falling nicely into place, except for one thing. The man Fred identified could not have been the killer. He had an airtight alibi for the night of the murder.

At the inquest into Norah's death, Fred had difficulty answering some routine questions. Why meet the stranger at Piccadilly Station? Wouldn't the shop have been a more convenient location? Why give a stranger the keys to the shop in the first place? How did Fred so enthusiastically and positively identify the wrong man?

The inquest jury brought in a verdict of "Willful murder against some person unknown." It was clear that Fred was suspected of the crime, and it was just as clear that there was no hard evidence against him.

Two long years went by. On July 25, 1933, Fred Field walked into a newspaper office and gave a detailed confession of how he had lured Norah Upchurch into the empty shop and strangled her to death. Fred said that he had robbed her of the few pounds she carried in her purse.

The wheels of justice turned ever so slowly. Fred was arrested and charged with murder. He was committed for trial at the Old Bailey, but when charged before the magistrate, he almost brought the house down when he stated loud and clear, "I plead Not Guilty, and reserve my defense."

Once his trial began, Fred explained that for two long years he had been scorned by his friends. They all thought he was a murderer. He couldn't stand it any longer. Now he insisted on being proven innocent or guilty in a court of law. The only way he knew to bring himself to trial was to confess to the murder.

Naturally his confession was a complete fabrication. Fred stated that he didn't want to go through life being known as the man who got away with murdering that poor unfortunate girl.

A man confessing to murder to prove his innocence; the story was fantastic enough to be believed. After some brief consultations everyone agreed that a guilty verdict would be impossible to arrive at with the existing evidence. The judge directed the jury to return a verdict of Not Guilty.

Fred walked out of the Old Bailey a free man. He joined the R.A.F. as an aircraftman in 1933, and for the next three years the world heard nothing of Mr. Frederick Field.

* * *

In April, 1936, the nude body of Mrs. Beatrice Vilna Sutton was found in her flat at Clapham. She had been strangled to death. At this time our old friend Fred was missing from his R.A.F. unit stationed at Hendon. On the very night Beatrice was murdered, April 4, Fred had shown up at the flat of a lady acquaintance. The girl's mother, who was present at the time, later stated that Fred behaved irrationally and had a wild look in his eyes. She said that Field had told them they would be reading about him in the newspapers. The woman, who was aware of Fred's past, called the police and reported Fred as a deserter from the R.A.F. She explained that she had made the call to protect her daughter. At the time she was unaware that the undiscovered body of Beatrice Sutton lay on a bed in Clapham.

Fred was picked up by the police and gave them a detailed confession of how he had strangled Beatrice. He revealed intimate details of the room where the murder had been committed, which only the killer could know.

Again, Fred stood trial for murder at London's Old Bailey.

Only the jury were unaware of Fred's past appearance. It was a shock to all when Fred stated once again that he had only confessed to assure himself of a day in court in order to clear his name. At the time of Beatrice's murder he was on the run as a deserter. Fred knew Beatrice, she let him sleep in a small cupboard off a hall outside her flat. Fred claimed that on the night of April 4, he saw a man running from Beatrice's flat. He walked inside the open door and discovered Beatrice's nude body.

Fred knew that if he called the police he would be suspected. Later, when he was picked up, he thought he would kill himself. What better way to do it than to confess to a murder and have the Crown execute him. Now, of course, he had thought better of the whole matter and was repudiating his confession. If the jury would just return a verdict of Not Guilty, he would be on his way.

This time Fred's confession was too detailed for his own good. He had gone to the well once too often. The jury deliberated only 20 minutes before finding him guilty.

Fred, who had thought up one of the most unique defenses ever conceived, was hanged for his crimes.

FAT MARTHA AND RAYMOND

Nineteen-forty-seven was not a good year for Martha Beck. Her husband had just divorced her and to make matters worse, she lost her job as a nurse at a home for crippled children in Pensacola, Florida. Fate had left her with two children; one sired by her former husband and the other the result of a tryst with a bus driver.

Martha had been willing to marry the bus driver, but unfortunately he had an aversion to settling down, particularly with Martha. You might call it an absolute phobia, because the bus driver took a step which assured him that no marriage would take place. Rather than marry Martha, he committed suicide.

You see, Martha was not a raving beauty. She was of average height, but that is about all that was average about her. Tipping the scales at 203 lbs., Martha had an array of chins and extra slabs of blubber that she wasn't even using. She was inclined to wear bright red lipstick, and overindulged her ample face with layers of rouge, which gave her an overstuffed, ghostlike appearance.

Martha had those normal urges which ladies sometimes have and longed for the company of a man. Facing the fact that she was no cutie she joined a Lonely Hearts Club. Before long she received a letter, which read:

Dear Martha,
   I hope you will allow me the liberty of addressing you by your Christian name. To tell the truth, I don't quite know how to begin this letter to you, because I must confess, this is the first letter of this sort that I have ever written.
   Would you like to know a little about me? I am 31

and I've been told I'm not a bad looking fellow. I am in the importing business from Spain, my mother country. I live alone here in this apartment, which is much too large for a bachelor, but I hope some day to share it with a wife.

Why did I choose you for my debut friendship letter? Because you are a nurse, and therefore I know you have a full heart with a great capacity for comfort and love.

Your friend,
Raymond Fernandez.

Martha didn't know it, but Raymond Fernandez was having a busy year as well. He was a swindler and killer who worked the Lonely Hearts Clubs. Once Raymond met, seduced, and got his hands on a lady's available funds, he disappeared leaving the poor woman dabbling at her bloodshot eyes with the corner of a handkerchief. When absolutely necessary he killed his victims.

Raymond was a very busy boy. He had just returned from Spain where had gone vacationing with a Jane Thompson. Jane unfortunately, didn't come back to the U.S. It seems she met with a car accident in La Linea, Spain. Fernandez had all the documentation concerning her death. He even had her last will and testament. Naturally it left the contents of her apartment to none other than Raymond Fernandez.

And so at Raymond's invitation, Martha went to visit him in New York. Raymond, always frugal, had moved right into the late Jane Thompson's apartment. My, my, what a surprise Raymond had when he threw open his front door and there stood the overstuffed, over-rouged, over-lipsticked Martha. Raymond gulped and said, "Come on in."

Fernandez was repulsed at the sight of Martha, but she thought he was an absolute heartbreaker. She fell madly in love with Raymond at that very first meeting. Not one to let grass grow under her bed, she let Raymond have his way with her the very first time they laid eyes on each other. Raymond, in his experienced way, checked out Martha's assets, and all things considered, decided to give Martha what they used to call the cold shoulder. Martha would have none of it. In desperation Raymond decided to tell her the truth, namely, that she was falling for a con artist and killer. You can imagine his surprise when Martha professed undying love for him in spite of his wayward habits. She even went so far as to suggest that they should become a team. She would pose as his sister, and instill confidence into the ladies he proposed to fleece.

Raymond warmed up to the idea and the partnership was formed. From the very beginning the Spaniard and the fat lady were a perfect combination. Raymond would correspond with lonely ladies, mostly widows, through several Lonely Hearts Clubs. Once contact was established, usually instigated by the ladies themselves, Raymond and Martha would show up at the mark's house. The unsuspecting victim would be impressed with Raymond and appreciative of his honorable intentions on lugging his sister along with him. After they got their scheme rolling, the odd couple averaged one fleecing a month.

There was one fly in the ointment. Martha was almost driven crazy with jealousy. She couldn't stand the thought that her Raymond had to caress and make love to other women. Raymond assured her that it was just part of his chosen profession and that it meant nothing personal.

Business is business, as the saying goes, and the partnership continued on its merry way. One incident is worthy of note. Raymond and Martha had made contact with a 66-year-old widow, Janet Fay of Albany, New York. After Raymond had seduced her and gotten his hands on Mrs. Fay's life savings of $6,000, Martha wanted to leave her high and dry. It appeared to Martha that Ray was lingering a little too long after the money was safely in his hands.

In a jealous rage Martha hit Mrs. Fay over the head with a hammer. Ray finished the job by strangling her with a scarf. Martha was later to state that she and Ray made love on the floor beside the body of their victim.

The following day Fernandez bought a trunk and placed the body of Mrs. Fay inside. He then managed to store the body at a friend's house for a few days. Raymond and Martha located a house for rent at 149th St., Ozone Park, Queen's, and took it on a trial basis for one month. They dug a hole in the basement, placed Mrs. Fay's body inside, and cemented the floor over. They remained in the house for four days until the cement dried. Then the odd couple moved out, informing the real estate agent that the house was unsuitable.

In this way they effectively disposed of Mrs. Fay's body.

Out of sight out of mind—the strange pair went on their merry way. Six weeks later they made contact with a widow from the suburb of Grand Rapids, Mich. Mrs. Delphine Downing had lost her husband two years previously. She was leading a lonely existence, raising her three-year-old daughter Rainelle by herself.

Soon Raymond and Martha visited Mrs. Downing at her invitation. In his usual charming way, Raymond made friends with little Rainelle. Then, following his regular script and drawing on his vast experience, he seduced the lonely Mrs. Downing. She became so enthralled with her lover and his large sister that she invited them both to move in with her and Rainelle. Raymond added to his role of lover and took on the extra responsibility of financial advisor. He and Mrs. Downing soon contemplated wedding bells. Raymond got busy converting her worldly assets to his name in anticipation of their impending marriage.

It appeared that Mrs. Downing could be the source of future concern for Raymond and Martha, so one fine day Raymond shot her in the head. Rainelle kept crying, and as a result made Martha nervous. Martha cured her nervousness by strangling the child. That same night Raymond dug a hole in the cellar. Here he placed the two bodies and poured cement into the hole. To relax after a hard evening's work, Raymond and Martha took in a movie.

The next morning, when neighbors couldn't get a satisfactory answer as to Mrs. Downing's whereabouts, they didn't hesitate to call the police. The authorities just couldn't believe that a woman who had lived in the same house for years would leave with her daughter, and not tell her future husband where she was going. They decided to search the house, and lo and behold they discovered that damp patch of cement in the basement.

Once the bodies of Mrs. Downing and Rainelle were uncovered, both Raymond and Martha poured out the whole horror story. They led police to the exact location in Queen's where the body of Mrs. Fay was buried under cement in the basement. As the house was now rented to new tenants, we can only speculate how they felt when informed that there was a body buried in their basement.

The authorities decided to extradite the pair from Michigan to New York State and charged them with murder. Michigan had abolished capital punishment while New York still retained the ultimate penalty.

Both were found guilty. On March 8, 1951, in the company of a Roman Catholic priest, Raymond was executed in the electric chair in Sing Sing Prison. Twelve minutes later Martha joined him.